18. 27
AM

50967

D1544147

50967

"BEHIND BAYONETS"

"There is something behind bayonets . . . the affections of home—the prayers and blessings of the family circle—the active assistance of the women and children left at home.

—MAJ. GEN. JAMES A. GARFIELD

DAVID VAN TASSEL, WITH JOHN VACHA

"Behind Bayonets"

The Civil War in
Northern Ohio

Published in cooperation with
the Western Reserve Historical Society

The Kent State University Press
Kent, Ohio

PUBLICATION OF THIS BOOK WAS SUPPORTED BY A GRANT FROM
THE CLEVELAND FOUNDATION

Library of Congress Catalog Card Number 2005016055

ISBN-10: 0-87338-850-X
ISBN-13: 978-0-87338-850-4

Manufactured in the United States of America

10 09 08 07 06   5 4 3 2 1

Library of Congress Cataloging-in-Publication Data
Van Tassel, David D. (David Dirck), 1928–2000
Behind bayonets : the Civil War in northern Ohio / David Van Tassel, with John Vacha.
    p. cm.
"Published in cooperation with the Western Reserve Historical Society."
Includes bibliographical references and index.
    ISBN-13: 978-0-87338-850-4 (pbk. : alk. paper) ∞
    ISBN-10: 0-87338-850-X (pbk. : alk. paper) ∞
    1. Ohio—History—Civil War, 1861–1865.   2. Ohio—History—Civil War,
    1861–1865—Pictorial works.   3. Ohio—History—Civil War, 1861–1865—Social
    aspects.   4. United States—History—Civil War, 1861–1865—Social aspects.   5.
    Cuyahoga County (Ohio)—History, Military—19th century.   6. Cuyahoga County
    (Ohio)—Social conditions—19th century.   I. Vacha, John.   II. Western Reserve
    Historical Society.   III. Title.
E525.V36 2005
973.7'09771—dc22   2005016055

British Library Cataloging-in-Publication data are available.

Contents

Foreword

BY EMILY VAN TASSEL

DAVID VAN TASSEL DEVOTED HIS CAREER to the promotion of historical understanding and public education. He wrote his first book on how Americans had invented themselves in part through how they chose to record their history. After his retirement, he planned to return to a manuscript that he had been working on, off, and on for several decades, which would have brought his first book, *Recording America's Past*, through to the end of the twentieth century. However, as he was fond of quoting, "the best laid plans. . . ." This, then, is his final book. It is a continuation of his exploration of how we as a people have used history to express who we are and who we wish to be.

History education was the driving force in my father's professional life. He cared deeply about his students and was known to get projects funded at times specifically to provide employment for graduates when history jobs were scarce. He promoted the study of history in secondary schools as well as in college, creating the National History Day competition that has touched millions of students and sparked in many of them an abiding interest in the past. He, along with John Grabowski, pioneered the city encyclopedia with *The Encyclopedia of Cleveland History*, which has served as a model for several other city encyclopedias. He served as vice president for the Teaching of the American Historical Association and helped create several graduate programs in public history at Case Western Reserve University.

The exhibit upon which this book is based was for him an opportunity to see historical creation from two very different perspectives: first from the familiar side of looking over and analyzing the kinds of artifacts and recollections that Clevelanders chose to keep or record; and second from the recording side, in his curatorial role of putting the artifacts and recollections together into a meaningful story.

When going through my father's papers to turn over to the Western Reserve Historical Society, I came across transcriptions of notes taken in seminars he taught at the University of Texas in the 1960s. He had a different student act as secretary each week, with minutes to be provided to every other student. He explained to them that this was to be their first practical lesson in historiography: who writes the history shapes the history written. This book and exhibit represent that idea on many levels.

It was initially to be my task to complete the manuscript for this book after my father died. However, when I found it emotionally too difficult to proceed, John Vacha graciously stepped in and put the pieces together. My family and I are very grateful for what he has done.

Preface

I NEVER EXPERIENCED DAVID VAN TASSEL'S classroom persona, having taken my history degrees shortly before his arrival at Case Western Reserve University in 1968. As a secondary teacher, however, I soon met him at a local history contest he organized for area students in 1974. I witnessed its rapid growth into a state contest and then into what is now National History Day. I also became involved in another of his many projects, *The Encyclopedia of Cleveland History*, which played a significant part in developing my own interest in the writing of local history. According to his former student and later colleague, John Grabowski, "David had a way of getting people to say 'yes.'" Over the years there have been hundreds, perhaps thousands, who have said "yes" and have carried on the outgrowths of his vision. So, when John asked if I would undertake the completion of David's unfinished manuscript on the Civil War, I had to say "yes."

This book is a part of David's last project, the exhibit "Civil War, for God, Union and Glory," which he curated for the Western Reserve Historical Society shortly after his "retirement" in 1998. Late in his teaching career David developed an interest in the Civil War and offered a course on the topic at Case. When the Historical Society decided to mount an exhibit of its nationally renowned Civil War collection, David, a trustee of the Society, volunteered to curate it and prepare a catalog. The catalog was later recast as a complementary, follow-up monograph focusing more closely on the events behind the lines on the homefront. Instead of simply translating the exhibit into a textual format, David decided to use little-known archival material uncovered during his curatorial research to provide a new perspective on the war that derived from Cleveland and northeast Ohio. David felt that this would provide an interesting, fresh view of the conflict that would be especially appealing to a regional audience and at the same time convey to that audience the power of original source materials, be they excerpts from letters or diaries or reproductions of photographs that depict local scenes.

Tragically, his unexpected death in 2000 occurred before he was able to bring this new approach to completion.

At the time of his death, David had completed three parts of the present text (the prologue and chapters 1 and 2) and working drafts of two additional chapters (3 and 4). He also had accumulated three large boxes of source materials. After reviewing the draft of the manuscript, John Grabowski and I agreed that the project could be completed and, indeed, that it needed to be done because it made a definite contribution to its subject. What was needed were conclusions for the two unfinished chapters, a new summary chapter dealing with later developments in politics and business (chapter 5), and a concluding epilogue. While more might have been added, we decided to confine the new material to the minimum necessary to provide closure to what should remain essentially the work of David Van Tassel.

While we were unable to discover any outline among David's effects, there were numerous clues both in the completed text and the source materials as to where he might have gone with the remainder of the work. It was clear, for example, that he intended to conclude with the Lincoln funeral, probably in an epilogue to balance the opening prologue. He also had collected material on the Soldiers' and Sailors' Monument, which, considering what he had done with the Perry Monument dedication, suggested additional epilogue matter. At the time of his death, he had apparently been in the process of going through the Oliver H. Perry letters; this provided another connecting link for the added text. Therefore, with no intention of suggesting anything in the nature of the paranormal, I can say that I truly felt a sense of collaboration with David in completing this manuscript.

A number of individuals and institutions have made significant contributions to the realization of this project. The support of the Van Tassel family is gratefully acknowledged, as is the funding provided by the Cleveland Foundation for the publication of this volume. Illustrations and clerical work came from the Western Reserve Historical Society, where Janet Mallula and Ann Sindelar were especially helpful. First and last, the continued determination and encouragement of John Grabowski were essential in seeing this book through to publication. While no one can really bring into being the book David Van Tassel would have written, I trust this comes reasonably close.

John Vacha

A Pleasant
Place to Live

IN 1860 THE PORT OF CLEVELAND at the mouth of the Cuyahoga River was a forest of masts and twisted ropes, with lake schooners, steamboats, scows, and canal barges crowding the river beyond the terminus of the Ohio Canal at the end of Superior Street and around the sharp horseshoe bend in the river. The noise of the busy shipping area was loud, a combination of clanking steam engines, the hiss of escaping steam, the shouts of stevedores and sailors, as docking, unloading, and onloading went on ceaselessly throughout the day. The wail of train whistles and the clanging of bells added to the din with their announcements of the arrival and departure of passenger and freight trains to or from the wooden depots of six railroad lines concentrated in the port area.

Few visitors wrote about the working aspects of this prosperous commercial city; most, like the editor of the *Columbus Gazette,* wrote of the products of prosperity such as the new public buildings, residential areas, and civic amenities. "We have been to Cleveland," he told his readers, "the city of broad streets and stately avenues, of charming drives and romantic scenery, of rural taste and architectural beauty, and after a stirring, lively visit of three days, we became so nearly captivated that we were almost persuaded to sell out our earthly possessions, so as to invest all our capital upon the Lake Shore." He visited the public buildings, the Marine Hospital, the Post Office (Federal Building), and the new County Courthouse and City Hall, noting that the "City Council Chamber is a very pleasant place to transact public business, being fitted up with mahogany desks, sofas and cushioned chairs, and neatly carpeted." However, "the little antique, ancient Market House in Cleveland, way down upon the Cuyahoga river, we looked upon as about the hardest piece of public property there, and we propose . . . to swap off our Steam Fire Engine for the old antediluvian meat shop."

This "forest of masts and twisted ropes" at the mouth of the Cuyahoga River was not why Cleveland was known as "the Forest City," but it was indicative of the city's bustling commerce in 1860. Much of the activity was centered around the shipyards, which were responsible for building a large percentage of the Great Lakes carrier fleets. Local concerns, such as the Cleveland Iron Mining Co., ensured that some of the carrying trade would remain in the home port.

Like a true traveler he urged his readers, "Never say that you have been to Cleveland again without adding—stopped at the Angier."[1]

The editor of the *Cincinnati Gazette,* who had visited somewhat earlier, told his readers that "Cleveland is the most desirable town in the 'Great West' to live in. . . . The town is clean, tasteful, elegant and healthful; for vegetables, fruit and flowers it is preeminent—for groves, parks, and ornamental trees and shrubs, it is hardly surpassed by New Haven. . . . Her public and private schools are excellent; her medical college superior to any in the West, and the prevailing character of society is educational, moral and religious. It is, therefore, 'just the spot' for the man of moderate income, to live and educate his family."[2]

And many influential Clevelanders were determined to keep the city a pleasant place to live. In February 1860 the City Council proposed an ordinance to ban coal oil manufacturing within city limits, and in July the Cuyahoga County Grand Jury indicted "the Rail Road Iron Mill Company, as a nuisance, on account of smoky chimneys!"[3] Three years earlier the City Council had passed an ordinance "making it unlawful to pour any refuse[,] slops, filth, etc., into the Cuyahoga river within the city limits."[4] The city's fathers had even determined that Public Square would be a city park and in 1857 had ordered a three-foot fence to be erected around the square, cutting off traffic through the square on Superior and Ontario Streets.

These were efforts made by a prosperous merchantile class to protect a residential city, but their very success in building the means of trading and distributing goods—canals, packet lines and barges, lake steam freighters, and railroads—made the next step, industrialization, almost inevitable. In fact Edwin Cowles, the short, unprepossessing editor of the young Republican newspaper, the *Leader*, championed new industry in his editorials and ranted against all regulation that might inhibit industrial growth. In an August 10, 1860, editorial he charged that while much talk was heard in Cleveland on the subject of manufacturing, nothing much was done about it. "We continue to make nothing and buy everything," he wrote. "Cleveland is the great wool mart of the West, and yet every yard of woolens worn or sold here is imported. The facilities for iron manufacture are unsurpassed, but the business is barely commenced."[5]

Less than a year later, Cowles demanded that the City Council repudiate the ordinance prohibiting pollution of the Cuyahoga River within the city limits, "which, in effect, shuts off manufactories, refineries, &c., from being established upon the river banks. . . . To refuse to do it, is to pursue the same policy toward manufacturers that has diverted trade and business to other more favorable points, and has very greatly retarded the legitimate growth of our city. Our prosperity hereafter will be measured by our manufactures," predicted the editor. "Pittsburg [*sic*] is not a pleasant city, but under its dense smoke and its begrimed atmosphere, it has a substratum of manufactures that will enable it to bid

Beyond the business district clustered near the river, Cleveland's residential neighborhoods spread eastward. Still dominated largely by church steeples, the city's tree-lined "broad streets and stately avenues" were earning Cleveland its reputation as a kind of urban Elysium.

defiance to all ordinary panics or dull seasons. . . . Cleveland, on the other hand, indicts her rolling mills because they smoke, and prohibits coal oil refineries because they smell badly, and gets laughed at by all her sister cities."[6]

George B. Senter, Republican mayor, echoed these sentiments in his annual address to the City Council on April 8, 1861, in which he noted the lagging development of manufacturing in the city. Declaring that "no situation affords better facilities for remunerative manufacturing," he charged that "no where is the hand of wealth more tightly closed against manufacturing enterprises." The commercial establishment might have lost some political offices, but it still controlled the purse strings of capital. In the hope of evening the playing field, Mayor Senter urged the council "not to neglect the opportunity given you . . . by your power over privileges and taxation . . . to encourage the settlement among us of mechanics and manufacturers."[7]

But in September 1860 Clevelanders were focused on something more exciting than gloomy warnings about the slow growth of industry. They were looking forward to the long-planned dedication of the Perry Monument in Public Square, to take place Monday, September 10, on the forty-seventh anniversary of Commodore Oliver Hazard Perry's victory in the Battle of Lake Erie during the War of 1812. Business and civic leaders of the community planned to make it a national event that would show the city off to the rest of the country. Dignitaries, such as the governors of Ohio and Perry's native Rhode Island, a former Secretary of the Navy, and veterans of the naval battle, were to speak. There was to be a grand procession of bands and military units from all over Ohio and as far west as Chicago, and late in the day there was to be a reenactment of the battle just off the lake shore.

Much of the bottom land along the winding Cuyahoga River still bore a semi-bucolic aspect in the 1850s. While the Flats were still dominated by Cleveland's mercantile interests, the smokestacks of nascent industries were beginning to jostle for position. Advocates such as Mayor George Senter and *Cleveland Leader* editor Edwin Cowles called for more industry-friendly legislation.

"THE FLATS" IN 1857.

The planning paid off. Visitors and participants streamed into the city. Train stations were abustle, and the rooms of Cleveland's eighteen hotels were filled. At seven o'clock Monday morning, Gustavus A. Hyde, an engineer of the Cleveland Gas Light and Coke Company who was to march in the parade with other company employees, checked the weather. It was already bright and clear. He inspected the weather instruments in his backyard at 20 Lake Street and recorded the temperature (48° F), wind velocity (12 mph), and general weather conditions (dry and "partly cloudy"). He would do so again at 2 P.M. and again before going to bed at 9 P.M., as he had done for the past five years, and at the end of the month he would send off the monthly records to Dr. James Espy, meteorologist at the Smithsonian Institution in Washington, D.C. Hyde was a native of Framingham, Massachusetts, where he had developed his interest in scientific weather study. Coming to Cleveland in 1850, in 1855 he joined Espy's 120 volunteers scattered around the country who formed a national network of weather observers.

The opening parade began at 11 A.M., and the *Leader* reporter charged with covering the day's events was clearly dazzled by the affair. The "grand procession," he wrote, included "large delegations of Military, Masons, Odd Fellows, &c., from Cleveland and other cities and towns. . . . It was truly a most splendid pageant. The numerous Bands of Music made the air fairly tremulous with patriotic strains, and the echoes of bugle blasts were thrown from side to side as if the houses were pelting each other with musical notes." Contributing to the pageantry was a large American Express wagon "filled with boxes and packages, duly labelled and drawn by eight horses in ornamented harness." Not to be outdone, S. J. Wadsworth, local agent for Grover and Baker's sewing machines, outfitted another wagon with girls actually at work on the Grover and Baker machines. In keeping with the occasion, there was also a fully rigged ship towed along the route

Top left: As a former Secretary of the Navy, George Bancroft was an appropriate choice to deliver the dedicatory oration for Cleveland's Perry Monument in 1860. The Massachusetts Democrat is remembered today chiefly for his monumental and groundbreaking *History of the United States*. With an eye on current political developments, perhaps, he told Clevelanders that "the Union will guard the fame of its defenders and evermore protect our entire territory."

Top right: An engineer for the Cleveland Gas Light and Coke Co. by day, Gustavus A. Hyde moonlighted as an amateur meteorologist. He was one of 120 volunteers nationwide who sent local weather reports to the Smithsonian Institution in Washington, D.C.

Dedicated with great pomp and ceremony on the eve of the Civil War was the monument to Commodore Oliver Hazard Perry, victor at the Battle of Lake Erie in the War of 1812. It was originally placed in the very center of Public Square, which was fenced off from through-traffic in 1857 and renamed Monumental Park shortly after the dedication. Eventually the square resumed its old name, and the monument began a journey of several moves across the city.

on wheels. "The procession throughout was the finest thing of the kind ever seen in Cleveland, and was an hour passing a given point."[8]

When the parade reached Public Square, the governors of Ohio and Rhode Island headed the dignitaries on the platform in front of the statue, surrounded by their staffs, members of the Rhode Island legislature, old soldiers, and other invited guests. The Reverend Dr. G. B. Perry of Natchez, Mississippi, gave the invocation and led the crowd in the Lord's Prayer. Local sculptor William Walcutt then stepped up to his creation and, to the shouts and applause of the multitude, pulled the Stars and Stripes to reveal the bronze and marble monument.

American historian and former Secretary of the Navy George Bancroft delivered the principal address, speaking of those who had fought for the mortal existence of the nation and offered their lives in its defense. Such heroism deserved to be commemorated by works of art, he said, so that the evidence of their virtue might be ever in the eyes of the people. After further remarks on the progress and achievements of the state of Ohio, Bancroft concluded on a note prescient with the impending national crisis. "The Union will guard the fame of its defenders and evermore protect our entire territory," he proclaimed. "It will keep alive for mankind the beacon lights of popular liberty and power . . . and its mighty heart will thrill with delight at every true advance in any part of the world toward republican happiness and freedom."

"Such a glorious ovation has never been equalled in the West," wrote the *Leader*'s reporter, who declined to give an exact number but safely estimated the throng as "such a crowd as has never before been seen in Cleveland." (Other reporters made various estimates of the crowd, shamelessly exaggerated at from 75,000 to 100,000.) Following Bancroft, Dr. Usher Parsons gave an eyewitness account of the Battle of Lake Erie, and the "*identical blue jacket* which [Perry] wore during the engagement" was displayed from the stand. Later in the evening the mock battle was staged on the lake: eleven vessels, drawn off into two squadrons, engaged in the sham skirmish. "The artillery companies performed their part very well," said the *Leader*, "and the sullen booming of the cannon came over the water with a heavy sound, but far lighter than if the hearers had had fathers or brothers at the guns, and it was a real battle." (The only real casualty reported during the day was the death of an unknown man off the pier near the Cleveland and Erie Telegraph building. Plunging into the lake on a dare to retrieve his lost cap, he suddenly sank and drowned "although a thousand people were within a stone's throw of him."9)

Sculptor William Walcutt did not complete his Perry Monument group until 1869, when the figures of a midshipman and sailor boy were placed on either side of the pedestal below the main figure of the commodore. At about the same time a square, black, iron fence with lampposts at each corner was placed around the monument. A bronze casting was made in 1926 to replace the badly deteriorated marble original.

Looking less like the future U.S. senator than the young man-about-town that he was, Marcus Alonzo Hanna dropped out of Western Reserve College with the blessings of its faculty at the end of his freshman year. He went to work for his father's wholesale grocery and commission house while maintaining his interest in boating, horse racing, and social life.

Central High School was not only Cleveland's first public secondary school but the first such institution west of the Alleghenies. Established in 1846, it moved ten years later from Prospect Street into this new building on Euclid Avenue, west of Erie (East 9th) Street. Future senator Marcus A. Hanna was one of its most famous alumni; John D. Rockefeller was without doubt its most successful dropout.

Reporters who had come in from Philadelphia, Boston, New York, Columbus, Toledo, and Detroit wrote in glowing terms about the event. The reporter from Pittsburgh, however, was not impressed. With true competitive bravado he wrote in the *Pittsburgh Chronicle,* "Pittsburgh could get up ten times a more imposing [event] with five days notice, yet the Clevelanders have had months for preparation."[10] Most, however, agreed with Fannie Fern, one of the country's most popular female writers, who had arrived Saturday evening in time to note the number of people coming into the city from all around, including "any number of military companies and strangers from a distance bound on the same patriotic errand. Every hotel, and even private residences, were crammed to the last possible extent."[11] "The sun shone out brilliantly on Monday upon the beautiful city of Cleveland, swarming with red coats, and rustics, and civilians, to see the statue, of which they may well be proud, both on account of its intrinsic merit, and because it is the work of a native artist," reported Miss Fern. "It stands conspicuously in the park, its fine proportions in beautiful relief against the dense foliage. We saw Cleveland in holiday attire, it is true, but apart from that it impressed me most agreeably, with its gigantic shade trees and pretty streets and gardens."[12]

This idyllic self-image that Clevelanders created for the nation had already gained currency in the region. Families from farms and towns in Ohio, western New York, and Pennsylvania had pushed the population from a little over

17,000 in 1850 to more than 43,000 in 1860. Among these newcomers was the rising Hanna clan. In 1852 Leonard Hanna settled his family in a "substantial brick house" on Prospect Street and, with his brother Robert and a hometown friend, Hiram Garretson, formed the wholesale grocery and commission house of Hanna, Garretson & Company with a warehouse on River Street. The Hannas had worked in the successful family grocery business a few miles south of Youngstown in New Lisbon, a prosperous and growing crossroads town, until a failed canal project and the town's vigorous opposition to the intrusion of railroads doomed it to stagnation and decline. The young Hanna brothers succumbed to the lure of Cleveland with the exception of Joshua, who went off to Pittsburgh and became a broker.

Leonard's oldest son, Marcus Alonzo (Mark), was a reluctant migrant at first. The handsome, athletic, and gregarious fifteen year old had many friends in New Lisbon, including a girlfriend. After months of anguish he broke off the relationship and threw himself into the social life of Cleveland. He attended Central High School, then a one-story, cottage-like building on Prospect Street surrounded by bushes and shade trees and a picket fence, soon to be replaced because of the growing population by a three-story brick building on Euclid Avenue from

From humble quarters on Erie (East 9th) Street, the Erie Street Baptist Church eventually became famous in a later location as the Euclid Avenue Baptist Church. Pictured is the congregation's second church, purchased from Second Presbyterian Church and moved to the Erie Street site. As one of the trustees, young John D. Rockefeller helped raise $2,000 to pay off the mortgage. He maintained his connection with what became known as "Mr. Rockefeller's Church" for nearly the rest of his life.

which Hanna graduated in 1856. At the urging of his mother, he entered Western Reserve College in Hudson but stayed only a year before being suspended.

Later, as a U.S. senator from Ohio, Mark Hanna recalled his brief career in higher education in a speech delivered in 1901 at the seventy-fifth anniversary of the founding of the college. "I am neither a student nor a scholar, and it is with diffidence that I address this audience," he admitted. "My connection with the Western Reserve College reaches back as far as 1857. . . . I entered what was called the scientific class, in which a kind-hearted professor made things easy for me. There were five members of the class when I entered it. Later the number dwindled to three, and when I left there was not any."[13] According to Hanna, he had been a victim of his environment. "At my boarding house I fell in with a number of jolly sophomores, and they persuaded me to help them in getting out a burlesque program of the Junior oratoricals. In the division of labor it fell to my lot to distribute these mock programs. I well remember when the iron hand of Professor Young fell on my shoulder. 'Young man,' he said, 'what are you doing?' 'I am distributing literature and education,' I replied, 'at the expense of the Junior class.' Well, it was near the end of the term, anyway, and I went home. I told my mother I thought that I would go to work, and that I was sure the faculty would be glad of it."[14]

Mark went to work in his father's business as a roustabout and then as a purser on the company's small fleet of lake steamers—the *Manhattan, City of Superior,* and *Northern Light*—carrying passengers and freight. Work, however, did not seem to hamper his social life; he was seen at parties all over town, at the races—the Forest City track was the most popular—and as a member of the Ydrad Boat Club, which owned a long racing shell and held rowing contests along the shores of Lake Erie against its rival, the Ivanhoe Boat Club.

A younger schoolmate of Hanna's at Central High School was John D. Rockefeller. He was vastly different from Mark Hanna in every way, from background to personality. John D. was a tall, very serious-looking young man, ambitious and hardworking. His father was a traveling salesman, usually of patent medicine cures, as well as a jovial philanderer and bigamist. William Avery Rockefeller moved his family from western New York to Cleveland in 1853, attracted in part by the schools. Money was often short, so his wife, Eliza, and the younger members of the family lived with a relative in Strongsville, while young John D. lived in a boardinghouse while going to school in the city. He joined the Erie Street Baptist Mission Church, where he swept floors, arranged flowers, and taught Sunday school. In 1855 he dropped out of Central High. After a three-month course at Folsom's Business College and a job search of nearly a month walking from office to office in downtown Cleveland, on September 26 he finally landed a position as clerk in the Hewitt and Tuttle Commission House. It was a date he would later observe annually with solemn ceremony, raising the flag every September 26 at his estate in East Cleveland.

Young Rockefeller soon won a reputation as a scrupulous bookkeeper and shrewd money handler, as well as a tough bargainer. In 1858 his father, already maintaining a second growing family in Ontario, gave John some money and orders to build a house on Cheshire Street for his mother and siblings. John D. drew the plans, took eight bids from builders, chose the lowest bid, bought the materials, and watched every step of the construction—so closely that the builders lost money on the project. In 1859 John D. obtained a $4,000 personal loan from banker Truman P. Handy, and with Maurice B. Clark set up his own commission house business of Clark and Rockefeller with warehouses on River Street.

Now both Hanna and Rockefeller were engaged in wholesale trading, the lifeblood of this commercial city; but both were also of a new generation of entrepreneurs who would, during the Civil War, transform the city into a center of industry.

For nearly half a century John Malvin was one of Cleveland's leading black citizens. He arrived in 1831 after enduring harsh treatment in his native Virginia, even though technically free. Malvin was active in the underground railroad prior to the Civil War and helped recruit a company of black soldiers during the war. His autobiography, published a year before his death in 1880, has been called "the only important first-person narrative written by a Cleveland Negro in the nineteenth century."

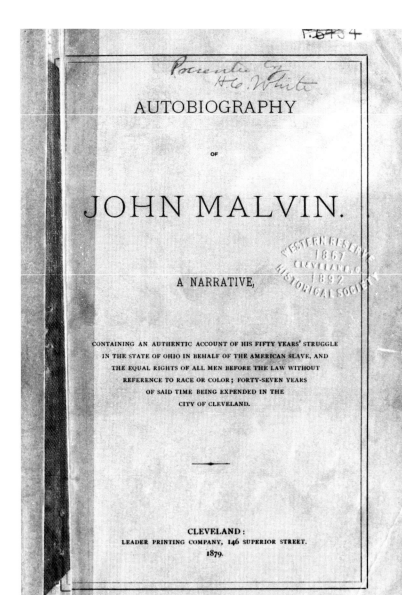

AUTOBIOGRAPHY

OF

JOHN MALVIN.

A NARRATIVE,

CONTAINING AN AUTHENTIC ACCOUNT OF HIS FIFTY YEARS' STRUGGLE
IN THE STATE OF OHIO IN BEHALF OF THE AMERICAN SLAVE, AND
THE EQUAL RIGHTS OF ALL MEN BEFORE THE LAW WITHOUT
REFERENCE TO RACE OR COLOR ; FORTY-SEVEN YEARS
OF SAID TIME BEING EXPENDED IN THE
CITY OF CLEVELAND.

CLEVELAND :
LEADER PRINTING COMPANY, 146 SUPERIOR STREET.
1879.

The Gathering Storm

THE IDYLLIC IMAGE PROJECTED BY the Perry Monument dedication of Cleveland as beautiful, prosperous, and united at the forefront of Western progress flashed briefly on the nation's consciousness. It was quickly obscured, however, by the victory of the strident new Republican Party after a hotly contested presidential campaign. The Republican Party embraced every activist group that had inspired social and economic turmoil during the decade following the Mexican War. It included Free Soilers, who opposed the extension of slavery into the territories gained in the war; members of the Liberty Party, who advocated outright abolition of slavery; temperance reformers and anti-immigrant members of the former American (Know-Nothing) Party; and finally the old Whigs, who favored protective tariffs to encourage industry and Federal subsidies for internal improvements. However discordant this mix of peoples and causes appeared to be, its constituents shared to one degree or another a common abhorrence for slavery.

Ohio was a "free" state by command of the Northwest Ordinance of 1787 and the first Constitution of the State of Ohio in 1803. And situated as it was across the Ohio River from the slave states of Kentucky and Virginia (after 1863, West Virginia), Ohio was a magnet to freedom-seeking runaway slaves. Once in Ohio, however, they found their expectations about the quality of freedom to be an illusion: the absence of slavery did not mean citizenship, racial equality, or even civility for blacks, free or fugitive. As one saddened fugitive put it,

> Ohio's not the place for me;
> For I am much surprised
> So many of her sons to see
> In garments of disguise.

Chorus:
Farewell, Ohio!
    I can not stop in thee;
I'm on my way to Canada
    Where colored men are free.

2. Her name has gone out through the world,
      Free labor—soil—and men—
    But slaves had better far be hurled
      Into the lion's den.

3. Ohio's not the place for me;
      An awful truth I state—
    They say they want the country free,
      But the colored man they hate.[1]

Benjamin Rouse had come to Cleveland in 1830 to organize Sunday schools in the Western Reserve for the American Sunday School Union. Among his many philanthropic activities, he aided in the formation of the Seamen's Friend Society and the First Baptist Church of Cleveland. Astute real estate speculations enabled him to build the three-story Rouse Block on Public Square.

While Ohio prohibited slavery, it was also under the constitutional obligation to recognize the Southern slave owner's right to retrieve his human property. Neither did it award its free black residents citizenship. In fact its legislature subsequently passed laws designed to discourage free black settlers, such as demanding a $300 bond and certificate of free status and prohibiting state tax money for schools that enrolled black students. This situation in effect made Ohio, with its network of canals and rail lines, simply a highway for an underground railroad bound for Canada. Nevertheless, some free and fugitive black Americans did settle in Ohio. Those that did tended to concentrate in the southern section of the state, closer to friends who may have preceded them or relatives whose freedom they may have hoped to purchase. Their presence probably exacerbated the anti-abolitionist proclivities of white Ohioans in southern Ohio, many of whom had emigrated from slave states themselves. Northern Ohio was settled largely by New Yorkers and New Englanders, however, and while not entirely free of race predjudice, they were relatively sympathetic (at least in principle) to the egalitarian sentiments of the Declaration of Independence.

John Malvin was a leader among Cleveland's small and diverse black community. He had seen firsthand the agonies of slavery. Born free in Virginia, he was apprenticed as a boy to a carpenter and, as he recalled, "I was treated little better than a slave myself. For my clothing, I was supplied every year with one pair of shoes, two pairs of tow linen pantaloons, one pair of negro cotton pantaloons, and a negro cotton round jacket," the roughest, cheapest product of the New England textile mills. "My food consisted of one peck of corn meal a week."[2] He recalled several beatings, one when he was caught attempting to run away: "My wrists were tied crosswise together, and my hands were then brought down and tied to my ankles; my shirt was taken off, and in that condition I was compelled to lie on the ground, and he began flogging me. He whipped me on one side till the flesh was all raw and bleeding; then he rolled me over like a log and whipped me on the other side in the same manner. When I was untied I put on my shirt. So severely was my flesh lacerated that my shirt stuck to my back, and I was unable to get it off without the assistance of an old lady who lived on the farm, who applied grease to it."[3]

The First Baptist Church of Cleveland reared this imposing brick edifice with its 150-foot spire in 1834 at the corner of Seneca (West 3rd) and Champlain Streets. Thanks largely to the influence of charter member John Malvin, a leader of Cleveland's small African American community, there was no provision for segregated seating in the new church. First Baptist later moved to East 9th and Euclid and eventually to Cleveland Heights; its original site is presently occupied by the Terminal Tower.

Malvin did get away to Cincinnati, where he worked as a carpenter, saved money, and met and married his wife, Harriet. He did not like the discrimination he found in Ohio and was determined to get to Canada, buy a farm, and be free. He and Harriet worked their way up the Ohio Canal, having to winter in Newark when the canal froze over. In the spring they continued to Cleveland, where they eventually decided to settle. Malvin worked as a cook for several months on a lake schooner and later as night engineer for a steam engine in a mill at the mouth of the Cuyahoga River.

Malvin joined a small group of Baptists in forming the first Cleveland Baptist Society. Among the handful of charter members were Benjamin and Rebecca Rouse, a couple from Massachusetts who had also recently settled in Cleveland, he as agent for the Sunday School Union and she as mother of their five children and zealous champion of humanitarian causes. Benjamin, a gregarious and hearty man, traveled the state successfully organizing Sunday schools. He also speculated in real estate and was sufficiently prosperous by 1852 to build a three-story brick office building on Public Square, which became known as the Rouse Block. The building often served as headquarters for several of Rebecca's crusading organizations. In the 1840s she had formed the Martha Washington and Dorcas Society for aid to the poor. In 1850 she organized the Cleveland Ladies Temperance Union and later in the decade the Protestant Orphanage Asylum.

When the Rouses, Malvin, and the other members of the small charter group of the Cleveland Baptist Society gathered enough numbers, they planned to build a church. The planners stumbled over the seating of the "colored members." When some suggested putting them up in the gallery, John Malvin objected vigorously, as he did to other schemes for segregation. As a charter member, Malvin's word carried weight, and with the support of other charter members the First Baptist on the corner of Seneca (West 3rd) and Champlain Streets was not segregated, nor was the Second Baptist Church (the Erie Street Mission Baptist Church), which Malvin also helped to found and which was later joined by John D. Rockefeller. By the late 1840s few of Cleveland's hotels, restaurants, or schools were segregated. This was owing in part to the geographic dispersion of the black population throughout the city and its small number (800 by 1860), one-third of whom were skilled workers.

While John Malvin could certainly take a share in the credit for ameliorating the situation of free blacks in Cleveland and in the state, he was but one of a number of politically active leaders. They included John Brown, a barber who accumulated a small fortune in real estate, and Madison Tilley, a contractor whose excavating business employed over 100 men. In 1853 they, along with others, including Oberlin graduate and journalist William H. Day, initiated a call for an "Ohio State Convention of Colored Freemen" that took place in January 1853 in Columbus. The delegates resolved that "as birth gives citizenship, we claim under

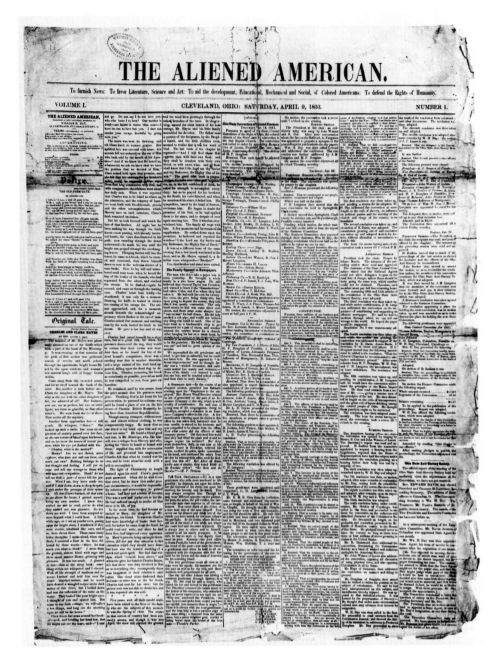

. . . the Constitution of this State, our rights as citizens: therefore, laws that have been, or may hereafter be passed, depriving us of citizenship, are unconstitutional, thereby null and void; and as we are taxed, we have and claim the right to vote."[4] The delegates also pledged to support a newspaper that would give them a voice; it would be established in Cleveland under the editorial leadership of William H. Day.

On Saturday, April 9, 1853, the first edition of *The Aliened American* appeared in Cleveland and was distributed all over Ohio and into some communities in New

Wanted by Federal authorities for his part in the massacre of pro-slavery settlers in "Bloody Kansas," John Brown returned to northern Ohio in 1859 to drum up support for the slave insurrection he hope to foment in Virginia. The Connecticut native spent most of his life in northern Ohio, where he had proved a failure in Hudson, Akron, and elsewhere. His final failure at Harpers Ferry, however, helped ignite the Civil War and made him a martyr to the Northern cause.

York, Pennsylvania, Michigan, Massachusetts, Connecticut, and western Canada. The paper's mission, Day announced, was "to visit weekly, the haunts and the homes of the sovereigns of this land, with our demand for simple justice: to aid the educational, mechanical and social development of Colored Americans: and while we furnish News—to favor Literature, Science, and Art. . . . So far as our principles are concerned, we commence, as we shall continue, independent: independent in religion—independent in politics—independent in everything;—the organ of no Party, and yet a Political paper; and the humble supporter of all good men." The articles preached self-help and communal cooperation, inspiration, hope, and offered models of manners, such as "a true gentleman . . . adds most manhood to his gentility; he depends, not upon his riches, nor the fineness of his cloth, but upon his intellect, his honesty and his truth." There were also articles that inveighed against the injustices done to free colored men. "The Black Man escaping from the savages of Slavedom, finds here discouragement, disfranchisement, prejudice, Negro-hate, in every nook and corner, of every locality, and almost in every individual wearing a sort of whitish skin," wrote corresponding editor Samuel R. Ward.[5]

That William Day gave effusive thanks for support from mainstream Cleveland newspapers, especially the *Forest City Democrat* and the *Herald,* both of which would become Republican organs (the *Forest City Democrat* became the *Cleveland Leader* in 1854), was indicative of the sentiments of many of the business, political, and religious leaders of the city. Officers of the Cleveland Anti-Slavery Society in the 1830s and later of the Cuyahoga County Anti-Slavery Society included John A. Foote, attorney and later a director of the Cleveland, Columbus & Cincinnati Railroad as well as of the Cleveland & Pittsburgh Railroad; Edward Wade, an attorney, leading abolitionist politician, and U.S. congressman; Solomon Severance, successful dry goods merchant; Rufus Spalding, state supreme court justice; Albert G. Riddle, lawyer and state legislator; Franklin T. Backus, attorney and state legislator; and J. M. Sterling, founder of the First Presbyterian Society. They shared the goal of "the entire abolition of slavery throughout the United States and the elevation of our colored brethren to their proper rank as men." The brutality of slavery was regularly brought home to northern Ohioans by traveling abolitionist lecturers sponsored by local antislavery societies and by a steady stream of fugitives moving through the villages and towns of northern Ohio on the underground railroad toward a promised land in Canada.

Such agitation inevitably led to violence, and northern Ohio's most famous abolitionist was also the most violent. John Brown of Hudson (not the barber) had dabbled in many businesses from tanning to sheepherding. He fathered nineteen children but otherwise had nothing to show for his fifty-six years of life except debts and many lawsuits. A lifelong opponent of slavery, he decided to become active in the cause and went to join two of his sons in the struggle for Kansas.

That territory had become a bloody battleground between settlers attempting to bring it into statehood as either a slave or free state. Brown carried out a raid on a pro-slavery settlement and butchered five of the settlers; he then fled to Canada, where he and a few supporters drew up a constitution that prohibited slavery and declared war on the institution in the South. Armed with this document and the designation of commander, John Brown toured Ohio and New England to raise money and recruits for his "Army of the Lord." He was frequently seen in the streets of Cleveland during the spring of 1859, telling his plans to any who might listen and become a recruit.

Then in October 1859 the *Leader* blared the news that John Brown had captured the Federal armory at Harpers Ferry, Virginia, and that members of his little army had been killed or captured by a detachment of U.S. Marines commanded by Col. Robert E. Lee. John Brown was taken prisoner, tried, and found guilty of treason and murder. With this, northern Ohioans began to see Brown not as a fanatical leader of the violent fringe of abolitionism but, now, as a martyr to the cause of freedom. Young James Garfield, teaching at the Hiram Polytechnic Institute, wrestled with his reactions to John Brown on the day of execution, Friday, December 2, 1859: "A dark day for our country. *John Brown* is to be hung at Charleston, Va. I have no language to express the conflict of emotion in my heart. I do not justify his acts. By no means. But I do accord to him, and I think every man must, honesty of purpose and sincerity of heart." Reflecting upon Brown's

Cuyahoga County's third courthouse was this imposing three-story structure raised in 1858, opposite the northwest corner of Public Square. Its first "celebrity trial" was that of the nineteen Oberlin slave rescuers in the spring of 1859. The third floor was also used as a "Museum and Fine Art Hall" for the Northern Ohio Sanitary Fair during the Civil War.

"devoted Christian character, his love of freedom drawn from God's Word, and from his Puritan ancestors, his sufferings in Kansas, his bold and daring courage, mixed with mercy, the human purpose of his heart in going to Virginia, his gallant treatment of those he had in his power, his neglect of his own safety, his frankness on the trial," Garfield could express nothing but empathy for the "gray-haired veteran standing on the fatal scaffold surrounded as he is at this moment by 2,000 American soldiers, and to ensure his death no friends to stand by him, who he is about to die because his heart beat for the oppressed. . . . Old Hero, Farewell. Your death shall be the dawn of a better day." In a small pocket diary under the same date Garfield simply entered "John Brown's Execution. *Servitium esto damnatum* [slavery be damned]."[6] The bells of all the Cleveland churches tolled slowly that afternoon to mark the hour of Brown's execution.

Earlier in the year Clevelanders had witnessed a fugitive slave case that also stirred the nation, the Oberlin-Wellington Rescue. The trial took place in the new Cuyahoga County Courthouse opposite the northwest quadrant of Public Square in the spring. It was the result of a dramatic rescue of a fugitive slave from Wadsworth's Hotel in Wellington, just forty miles from Cleveland. John Price, a fugitive slave from Kentucky, had worked in Oberlin almost two years when someone who had seen the reward posters notified John P. G. Bacon, his former master in Kentucky. Bacon then informed a Federal marshall from Columbus, who joined a pair of Southern slave catchers in Oberlin and lured John Price to the outskirts of town, where they seized him and took him in a carriage to Wellington, the closest stop on the Cleveland, Columbus & Cincinnati Railroad, to catch the next train for a hearing in Columbus. They commandeered an attic room in Wadsworth's Hotel to hold their captive while waiting for the train.

Meanwhile, witnesses sounded the alarm in Oberlin, and a reported 600 men headed to Wellington, nine miles south of Oberlin. Both town and gown were well represented in the headstrong exodus, which included businessmen, farmers, Oberlin College faculty and students, and the better part of Oberlin's substantial black population (about 400) on horseback, in carriages, and on foot armed with sticks, pitchforks, and some rifles. The angry mob surrounded the hotel and forced the marshall to give up his prisoner. Price was whisked away back to Oberlin, whence he was spirited on the underground railroad route to Canada. The rescuers made no secret of what they had done or of their identities. Consequently, witnesses identified many of them, and thirty-seven Oberlin and Wellington men were arrested and indicted for violation of the Fugitive Slave Act of 1850.

Three distinguished Cleveland attorneys with strong antislavery credentials volunteered their services for the defense of the rescuers. Judge Rufus P. Spalding, a former Ohio Supreme Court justice, pillar of the Presbyterian Church, and outspoken opponent of slavery and the Fugitive Slave Act, led the defense team. Albert Gallatin Riddle, nearly twenty years Spalding's junior, at age forty-

Opposite: Twenty of the Oberlin rescuers tried in Cleveland for violating the Fugitive Slave Act posed for their photograph in the courtyard of the Cuyahoga County Jail. Rejecting bail on principle, they were treated more as guests than prisoners by a sympathetic jailor. Simeon Bushnell and Charles Langston, the only two actually tried, stand ninth and twelfth from the left, respectively.

three, had already served as prosecutor for Geauga and Cuyahoga Counties and as representative in the state legislature. Franklin T. Backus, a former state senator, completed the initial team. All were active politicians. Spalding helped found the Cuyahoga County Republican Party, Riddle would run for Congress on the Republican ticket, and Backus ran for the Ohio Supreme Court.

On Tuesday, April 5, 1859, the trial of the first of the rescuers, a thirty-year-old Oberlin clerk named Simeon Bushnell, opened to a packed courtroom. Wives, relatives, and friends of the rescuers were in the audience, along with reporters from all of the major northern Ohio newspapers and some from as far away as New York and Massachusetts. The trial was clearly political, with the prosecutors, judge, and jury all Democrats and the defense all antislavery Republicans. The defense attorney's closing arguments played to the audience. Albert G. Riddle summed up his case with an indictment of slavery, as he said, "I know [the Fugitive Slave Act] is here held as law. That the decision of this Court is to add another scale to that great scab, that deforms and debauches American jurisprudence. . . . But it shall never be recognized and accepted by our people as law—never! never!!"[7]

Concluding for the defense, judge Rufus Spalding declared that "slavery is like a canker, eating out the vitals of our liberties, and . . . the Supreme Court of the United States has become the impregnable fortress and bulwark of slavery: I now say that unless the knife or the cautery be applied to the speedy and entire removal of the diseased part, we shall soon lose the name of freedom, as we have already lost the substance, and be unable longer to avoid confessing that TYRANTS ARE OUR MASTERS."[8] In less than two hours the jury came back with a verdict of guilty. Judge Hiram V. Willson said he would not hand down his sentence until

Judge Rufus P. Spalding headed the defense for the Oberlin rescuers. Antislavery views had led the former Democrat to aid in the organization of the Republican Party in northern Ohio. Later Spalding defended the escaped slave Sara Lucy Bagby in Cleveland and served three terms in the U.S. House of Representatives.

the completion of the next trial, which would begin Monday morning. The prosecutor demanded that the rest of the rescuers, who had been free on their own recognizance, now be taken into custody. Judge Willson set bail at $500. The rescuers, in caucus with their lawyers, decided that they would refuse to post bail or to be responsible for their own recognizance, and summarily they were marched off to the Cuyahoga County Jail around the corner from the courthouse.

It was clear from the beginning that they were to be treated like no ordinary prisoners. They were greeted at the door by the sheriff, who welcomed them as guests. Jailor John B. Smith gave over the use of his own apartment on the third floor for the rescuers' convenience in receiving guests, of which there were many. Ladies brought baskets of food. Ministers came pledging their support, as did politicians, legislators, and a large Sunday school class from Oberlin. Even John Brown paid a visit, tucking his patriarchal beard into his collar to avoid detection, since he was wanted by Federal authorities for his exploits in "Bleeding Kansas." Professor Henry B. Peck, a minister and rescuer, held Sunday services from the steps of the jailhouse for hundreds of supporters. Scarcely a day went by when there was not a protest rally somewhere in northern Ohio, and there were always protesters in front of the jail. The rescuers had their collective photograph taken in their Sunday best, standing in front of the jailhouse, by J. M. Green, one of Cleveland's best photographers.

The next rescuer to be tried was Charles Langston, a free black man and Oberlin student, school teacher, and recording secretary of the Ohio State Anti-Slavery Society, headquartered in Cleveland. Prosecution and defense followed the same pattern as in Bushnell's trial, with the same twenty-two witnesses for the prosecution. Fifteen court days later it ended with the same verdict. On Wednesday, May 10, Judge Willson sentenced Simeon Bushnell to pay a $1,000 fine and court costs, as well as to serve sixty days in jail. He then adjourned court until Thursday morning, when Langston would hear his sentence.

After court opened the next morning, Judge Willson asked Charles Langston if he had anything he wanted to say. Langston, a handsome, somber-looking man in his late thirties, rose to his medium height and told the judge he would like to speak. Then, addressing the jury and the audience, he gave an eloquent speech, frequently punctuated by applause, about the brutality of slavery and the injustices and indignities visited on his people. He concluded, "I was tried by a jury who were prejudiced; before a court that was prejudiced; prosecuted by an officer who was prejudiced, and defended, though ably, by counsel that were prejudiced. And therefore it is, your Honor, that I urge by all that is good and great in manhood, that I should not be subjected to the pains and penalties of this oppressive law, when I have not been tried, either by a jury of my peers, or by a jury that were impartial."[9]

Unmoved by the "great and prolonged applause" for the black man's oratory, Judge Willson said simply, "Still, the law must be vindicated" and proceeded to announce sentence: a $100 fine and court costs and twenty days in jail.[10] He then adjourned the court early to attend to the details of his daughter's wedding. The next trial would not be held until the opening of the next session in July. Audience, lawyers, rescuers, and the public were all incensed. The rescuers would have to remain in jail until the opening of the July session unless they posted bond, which they would not do and most could not afford anyway. Protest rallies continued in the towns of the Western Reserve. A huge rally in Cleveland was planned and advertised for Tuesday, May 24. Giant multicolored posters appeared everywhere, inviting people to come. The railroads were offering half-price fares for those who wished to attend the rally.

The morning of the rally promised a bright and balmy day. Hundreds of men and women began arriving by train. Thirteen packed cars arrived from Oberlin, heralded by a brass band. Trains also steamed in from Elyria, Columbus, Cincinnati, Toledo, and Pittsburgh. The Lake Shore Railroad brought in sixteen carloads of ralliers. Delegations from Lorain, Ashtabula, and Lake Counties were accompanied by more brass bands, and outside the depot they formed in line and marched to Public Square, flying banners with handpainted slogans. Fiery Joshua R. Giddings, congressman from Ashtabula, had organized an action group at a previous rally called Sons of Liberty, who marched under a banner proclaiming,

Sons of Liberty.
 1765.
Down with the Stamp Act!
 1859.
Down with the Fugitive Slave Act!

Crowds assembled in front of the jailhouse, over which flew a banner proclaiming in large letters, "Oberlin Wellington Rescue." Politicians spoke, rescuers spoke, Charles Langston stood on the rails of the fence outside the jail and whipped the crowd into a frenzy, as did Congressman Joshua Giddings. Governor Salmon P. Chase, a Republican presidential hopeful, was whisked in from Columbus at the last minute to calm the angry crowd, which threatened at any moment to break loose and storm the jail to free the rescuers.

The day did end peacefully, but Ohio Republicans were increasingly disposed to insist that something had to be done about the Fugitive Slave Act. The issue nearly split the Republican Party meeting in Columbus, the Resolutions Committee finally agreeing on a compromise calling for a plank in the national party platform strongly denouncing the Fugitive Slave Act but falling short of calling it unconstitutional. The rescuers, meanwhile, continued to entertain visitors through the rest of May and June. They even planned a biweekly newspaper entitled *The Rescuer,* for which only one number was ever issued—that of July 4. On July 6 charges against the rest of the rescuers were dismissed, and they were released from jail. Their release came as the result of a deal between Federal officials and Lorain County, which had returned indictments against the Federal marshalls and the Kentucky slave catchers for kidnapping. Both sides now agreed to back down. The Buchanan administration wanted no more of these demonstrations fueling the Republican cause.

The antislavery issues represented in the Oberlin-Wellington trial and the actions of John Brown and his trial inflamed radicals in both parties, Democratic and Republican, so that the nominating process in the spring and the presidential election campaign in the summer and fall of 1860 focused solely on slavery. Cleveland, long dominated by Democrats, was now overwhelmingly Republican as Whigs, Free Soilers, and Know-Nothings moved into the city and joined forces in the mid-1850s. Edwin Cowles, bellicose editor of the *Leader,* was one of the founders of the Republican Party in Cuyahoga County and an early supporter of Abraham Lincoln for president. He described the excitement as crowds around the telegraph office of the newspaper speculated on candidates, wagered, and waited for news from the Republican National Convention in Chicago.

"The excitement and impatience shown thro'out the city yesterday in regard to the Chicago news was intense," stated the *Leader* of May 19, 1860. "The customary salutation of 'How do you do?' was exchanged for 'Any news from Chicago?' and the telegraph and newspaper offices were beseiged from an early hour." The *Leader*'s office naturally became a focal point for the excitement, as men crowded

Occupying the center of the picture, to the left of the City Hotel, is the Cuyahoga County Courthouse with the adjoining, slightly taller jailhouse immediately behind. The jail annex was home for the Oberlin rescuers during the three months of their trial. Dominating the scene was the First Presbyterian Church.

Left: The first and only issue of *The Rescuer* was issued from the Cuyahoga County Jail on July 4, 1859. The editors asked for the indulgence of their readers, "As the entire work of editing and type-setting is to be done by prisoners within prison-walls, and therefore, not within reach of the facilities which usually promote such labor." Though projected as a biweekly, the newspaper was discontinued after this single issue when charges were dropped against the remaining Oberlin rescuers.

Right: A clean-shaven Abraham Lincoln headed the Republican presidential ticket in 1860. Cleveland Republicans donned oilcloth capes and paraded with kerosene torches in support of his campaign. *Plain Dealer* editor Joseph Gray remained unimpressed, writing that "a correct likeness of Mr. LINCOLN would be condemned as a caricature by anyone who did not know that was true."

the walk in front of a bulletin board waiting for the first telegraphic flashes, meanwhile discussing and betting on the chances of Seward, Lincoln, and Chase. Two days later the *Leader* reported the firing of 100 guns on Public Square by Artillery Company D in honor of the Republican presidential ticket of Abraham Lincoln and Hannibal Hamlin.

Joseph Gray, Democratic editor of the *Plain Dealer* and supporter of Senator Stephen A. Douglas, Lincoln's old Illinois rival, reported the split of the Democratic Party as a delegate to the failed Charleston, South Carolina, convention and the reconstituted northern Democratic Convention meeting in Baltimore, where Gray finally saw his candidate nominated. The ensuing campaign was bitter, nasty, and blatantly racist. No such subtleties as code words were for Joseph Gray, as he charged in a profile of Abraham Lincoln. "In personal appearance Mr. LINCOLN is long, lean and wiry," he wrote. "His complexion is about that of an octoroon. . . . A correct likeness of Mr. LINCOLN would be condemned as a caricature by anyone who did not know it was true."[11] In the August 18 edition of the *Plain Dealer* Gray announced that "An intelligent Darkey this morning gave it as his opinion that there were at this time one thousand stranger negroes in this city. The Republicans teach them to carry knives and rip their way to freedom, which advice they follow to the letter. . . . Give us LINCOLN for President, pledged to the 'Irrepressible Conflict' and the policy of freeing all the niggers . . . and the white men's lives would be in jeopardy every hour."

Cleveland Democrats put aside such fears, however, to celebrate the nomination of their anticipated deliverer, Douglas. "We never before heard such guns," described the *Plain Dealer*'s reporter. "Private citizens drank Roman Punch by the light of Roman Candles, and we noticed some very brilliant rockets to shoot up from near the mansion of our Democratic and German friend Judge HESSEN-MUELLER, which seemed to go to the very himmel."[12]

Clevelanders were active campaigners, joining Republican Wide-Awake clubs in every ward. Members sported a uniform consisting of an oilcloth cape with a gold stripe down the middle and a kerosene oil torch at the end of a pole. The Democratic counterparts called themselves the Little Giants. Both sides drilled, lit up parades for party rallies, and got out the vote on election day.

Republicans swept northeast Ohio and all but two wards in Cleveland. Lincoln won a majority in almost every county of northeast Ohio. The victory also swept in Republican Albert G. Riddle as the congressional representative of the Nineteenth District, and a Republican majority took City Council. The victory celebration in Public Square was tumultuous. "There was shouting, cheering, laughing and applause, such as only a vast multitude, excited and imbued with one common enthusiasm can get up," reported the *Leader*. "They brought out the artillery companies with their guns and one hundred thunderous echoes of the popular voice told to all town and country that Lincoln was elected." The Wide-Awakes visited city leaders and "finally at 5 o'clock, while the light of the bonfires flashed back from their torches, and the streaks of dawning light in the east began to shoot up into golden liberty poles, and every body was hoarse with their exultant shouts for Lincoln and victory, and empty stomachs yearned for breakfast, the Wide Awakes filed away to their torch rooms and the day broke over as great a night of rejoicing as Cleveland has ever seen."[13]

Lincoln's sweep of the Northern states decided the election but left the country more divided than ever. He failed to carry a single slave state, most of which voted for their own sectional candidate, John C. Breckinridge. Although Lincoln won a plurality of the popular vote, the combined Democratic vote for Douglas and Breckinridge was half a million more than the Republicans'.

"It will be a short war"

CHAPTER 2

No sooner had the smoke and noise of the all-night Republican celebration of Lincoln's election victory cleared from Public Square than Clevelanders read with mixed anger or concern, but rarely indifference, the news that South Carolina was planning to secede from the Union. Throughout November and early December, the *Leader,* the *Herald,* and the *Plain Dealer* reported on the progress of the secession convention meeting in Charleston, South Carolina, with imprecations such as "traitor" and concerns that they "know not what they are doing" in the Republican journals to the *Plain Dealer*'s insistence that they were honest men who were defending the Constitution against Republican radicals. Clearly, many people thought nothing would come of all this posturing, that Congress would come up with yet another compromise, and that President James Buchanan's moderate "wait and see" policy would prevail.

Thanksgiving in Cleveland was traditionally a quiet and religious holiday, but parishioners all over town were now treated to fiery sermons on the necessity of protecting freedom. At last, on December 20, the news broke with a one-sheet extra of the *Charleston Mercury* that announced in black, bold headlines, "UNION IS DISSOLVED!" and declared that there was "passed unanimously at 1:15 o'clock, P.M., December 20th, 1860, an ordinance To dissolve the Union between the State of South Carolina and other States united with her under the compact entitled 'The Constitution of the United States of America.'"

The next day, the *Plain Dealer* screamed "SOUTH CAROLINA OUT OF THE UNION—The Act of Secession Passed the Convention by a Unanimous Vote." Editor Joseph Gray declared, "The compact which our fathers, dripping with the blood of the Revolution, made, and which has created us a great, prosperous, and powerful nation, is broken, and our boasted Nationality is gone." Gray, who had campaigned for Douglas in the South, warned, "They are in earnest, dead earnest,

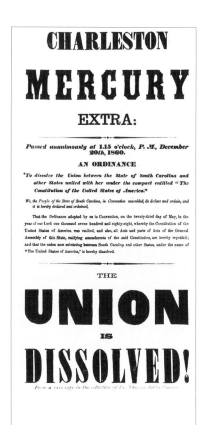

CHARLESTON

MERCURY

EXTRA:

*Passed unanimously at 1.15 o'clock, P. M., December
20th, 1860.*

AN ORDINANCE

"To dissolve the Union between the State of South Carolina and
other States united with her under the compact entitled "The
Constitution of the United States of America."

We, the People of the State of South Carolina, in Convention assembled, do declare and ordain, and
it is hereby declared and ordained,

That the Ordinance adopted by us in Convention, on the twenty-third day of May, in the
year of our Lord one thousand seven hundred and eighty-eight, whereby the Constitution of the
United States of America was ratified, and also, all Acts and parts of Acts of the General
Assembly of this State, ratifying amendments of the said Constitution, are hereby repealed;
and that the union now subsisting between South Carolina and other States, under the name of
"The United States of America," is hereby dissolved.

THE

UNION

IS

DISSOLVED!

From a rare copy in the collection of Dr. Thomas Addis Emmet.

With this simple one-page broadsheet that did little more than reprint South Carolina's Ordinance of Secession, the *Charleston Mercury* announced in effect that the Civil War had been inaugurated. Ten additional Southern states would follow suit over the next few months. Before the struggle was over, some Southern newspapers, due to the Northern blockade, would be reduced to issuing their extras on the back side of wallpaper sheets.

and are driven by a public opinion as irresistible as that which controls all public men in these fiery Northern Abolition States."[1]

Meanwhile, through December Clevelanders could do nothing but go about their business, which continued its recovery from the Panic of 1857. The new commission house of Clark, Rockefeller and Gardner, although only a little over a year-and-a-half old, was doing a thriving business. Young John D. Rockefeller was exhilarated by the profits his new firm was making. He later recalled that when he went to bed in such a mood he would chide himself, "Now a little success; soon you will be thrown down, soon you will be overthrown. Because you have got a start, you think you are quite a merchant. Look out, or you will lose your head—go steady!"[2] Rebecca Rouse was also taking advantage of the business recovery to raise money, though not for profit. As president of the Protestant Orphanage Society, she had just led a successful drive for a new orphanage building.

From Cleveland's perspective, after the new year the situation in the South grew more and more ominous as, one by one, Georgia and the Gulf states took themselves out of the Union. To Edwin Cowles, editor of the *Leader,* war was clearly imminent, and some Clevelanders were preparing for the worst. Volunteer militia groups such as the Cleveland Grays, the Hibernian Guard, and the new German company began to gather recruits and drill so that they would be able to offer their services if called upon.

Amid the uncertainties surrounding the transfer of power on the national scene, another fugitive slave case, that of Sara Lucy Bagby, threatened to inflame the city and give added ammunition to secession in states still debating their withdrawal from the Union. On Saturday, January 19, 1861, a U.S. marshal, the county sheriff, and a deputy called at the house of L. A. Benton, a jeweler who resided at 151 Prospect Street, and demanded the surrender of the "fugitive Lucy." Lucy Bagby had been working for Benton as a domestic servant for the previous two weeks and before that for congressman-elect Albert G. Riddle. She had run away from William Goshorn of Wheeling, Virginia. Someone in Cleveland, seeking a reward, got word to Goshorn about Lucy's whereabouts, and Goshorn asked the U.S. marshal to return her. The marshal took Lucy into custody and ordered the sheriff to hold her in the county jail. Benton, presumably, notified judge Rufus Spalding, who immediately agreed to act as her attorney. Spalding applied to the Common Pleas Court for a writ of habeas corpus, which probate judge Daniel R. Tilden granted, ordering Lucy to be brought before his court at 2:00 on Sunday afternoon, January 20.

Although Cleveland had outgrown the earlier custom of church bells sounding the alarm when "slave catchers" were spotted in town, word of mouth spread the news almost as rapidly, and crowds began to gather in front of the courthouse and in the jail yard Sunday morning. By one o'clock the crowd had become so large and surly that police drove them out of the jailhouse yard, blacks and

Sara Lucy Bagby became one of the last blacks returned to the South under the Fugitive Slave Act when she was discovered after her escape from western Virginia to Cleveland. Though angry crowds protested her arrest and trial, the city forbore any rescue attempt as a demonstration to the seceding Southern states that the hated fugitive laws could be enforced in the North. Freed during the Civil War, "Miss Lucy" eventually returned to live in Cleveland.

whites, men and women alike. However, they were already jamming the halls and stairways of the courthouse, waiting for the arrival of Lucy and the opening of the courtroom. Shortly before 2:00 P.M. the courtroom doors opened and the crowd spilled in, filling the room to overflowing. Judge Tilden, seeing the size and sensing the mood of the crowd, ruled that it would be unnecessary and "imprudent" to bring Lucy to the courthouse for the hearing. The question did not directly involve the prisoner, since it revolved around the issue of whether a U.S. marshall could order a local sheriff to hold in jail a fugitive slave who had committed no crime against the state. Judge Tilden had reviewed the Ohio law and ruled that

Above: Edwin W. Cowles, editor of the *Cleveland Leader*, had been one of the founders of the Republican Party. An outspoken opponent of slavery, his counsel in favor of nonviolence in the Bagby fugitive slave case stuck in his craw. A survivor from the era of personal journalism, Cowles was said to have always carried a pistol with which he practiced marksmanship on a target hanging in his office.

Right: Presiding over the Bagby fugitive slave hearing, U.S. commissioner Bushnell White offered to start a fund for the slave's purchase but was reluctantly constrained to order her return to the South. White in private life was one of the "Arkites" who gathered in a cabin near Public Square to study and discuss history.

Lucy could not be kept in jail, and thus the U.S. marshall would have to detain her elsewhere until her trial.

Marshall Matthew Johnson had a room fitted up for Lucy in the Post Office Building, a Federal facility on the other side of Public Square. The actual fugitive slave hearing was postponed for two days to give Judge Spalding time to gather whatever evidence he could uncover in Wheeling. The issues to be determined were whether William Goshorn could prove that he owned a slave by the name of Sara Lucy Bagby and whether the defendant was indeed that slave.

In granting Spalding's request for a recess, U.S. commissioner Bushnell White intimated that Lucy's owners viewed the proceeding as a test case to see whether the Fugitive Slave Act could be enforced in the notoriously antislavery Western Reserve. "The citizens have shown a disposition to maintain order, and if we wait, I think this disposition will be increased," stated the commissioner. "I wish to show the South that a law as distasteful to us, as a law against the slave trade is to them, can be carried out here; and that . . .we are true and loyal to the constitution."[3] Though Goshorn had indicated a disinclination to sell his slave before she had been legally returned to him, the *Leader* nonetheless announced that it would receive contributions for the purchase of Miss Lucy's freedom at the newspaper's counting office.[4]

Upon resumption of the hearing two days later, Judge Spalding rose to announce his failure to obtain any evidence to controvert Goshorn's claim of ownership. "May it please the Court," he said, "the time has arrived when I feel myself in duty bound to surrender my unfortunate client to the demands of that law, 'whose tender mercies are cruelties.'"[5] While offering $100 himself toward her purchase, Commissioner White carried out his "unpleasant duty" of ordering Lucy to be returned to Wheeling by the next train.

In order to ensure safe passage and prevent rescue attempts, the sheriff had sworn in 150 new deputies, who, armed with truncheons, surrounded the carriage containing the marshall and his prisoner and moved slowly through the crowded streets to the Erie Street station of the Cleveland & Pittsburgh Railroad. The party boarded without incident, but there was a plan to rescue Lucy from the train. Two suspicious-looking men, one black and the other white, reported the *Leader,* boarded the train at Ravenna. They were searched, and the black man was found with an iron bar that he had intended to use to uncouple the car in which the prisoner was riding when the train reached the next town, where a crowd waited to whisk her away. The engineer, having been alerted and seeing the angry crowd of armed men awaiting the train, slowed down as if to stop but then speeded up, foiling the plan and missing the scheduled stop at North Lima, Ohio.[6] Lucy Bagby thus became possibly the last slave surrendered in the North under the Fugitive Slave Act, though her reenslavement proved of short duration. Early in the Civil War, Union troops marched into Wheeling and restored her freedom.

Clevelanders got a chance to see Abraham Lincoln's newly grown beard when the Republican president-elect stopped in the city on his way from Illinois to his inauguration in Washington, D.C. Shortly after leaving Cleveland, in fact, Lincoln got a chance to meet the young girl who had first suggested the whiskers, when his train passed Westfield, New York (the girl's hometown), on its way to Buffalo.

In the immediate aftermath of the case, Cleveland and the *Leader* came in for scathing criticism from the abolitionist *Ashtabula Sentinel:* "So it would seem that . . . Goshorn did not really want the poor human being they called their slave, but they wished to see if they could make the Western Reserve eat dirt, and swallow all the resolutions they had ever passed on the subject of this damnable Fugitive Slave Law. It must be very pleasant to the citizens of Cleveland to be thus made the dirt eaters for the whole Reserve."[7] Replied Editor Cowles in the *Leader,* "When we have another fugitive slave case we shall take pains to telegraph the editor of the *Sentinel* and give him an opportunity to practice what he preaches by coming up and resisting." Defending the city, Cowles added, "Nothing would have given more 'aid and comfort' to seceding traitors of the South than a rescue here in Cleveland. That aid and comfort we did not care to give, and could do no less than advise non-resistance in this case."[8]

Meanwhile, the Fugitive Aid Society, which met regularly at the Methodist Church on Bolivar Street and was the public face of the underground railroad, was actively looking for the informer. It caught William R. Ambush, a black man, and charged him "with complicity in procuring the return of the fugitive slavegirl Lucy to her master."[9] At a late-night meeting in the Methodist Church, however, the "vigilante committee" exonerated Ambush. It seems he had received a letter from Pittsburgh in December saying that Goshorn was looking for Lucy.

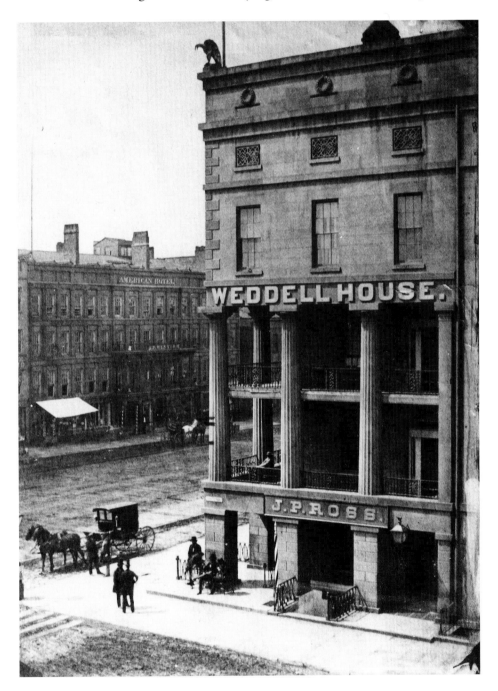

Opened in 1847, the Weddell House's proudest moment occurred when president-elect Abraham Lincoln stayed there on February 15, 1861. He spoke to a large crowd from a platform extending from the hotel's recessed balcony, which dominated the intersection of Superior Avenue and Bank (West 6th) Street. With its four-story addition running along Bank Street, the 300-room Weddell House was Cleveland's principal hotel in the Civil War era.

He proved that he had informed Lucy and that she had chosen not to "escape."[10] Thus the matter rested. Cleveland had averted a mob rescue and a repeat of the Oberlin-Wellington trial, salving its collective conscience with the knowledge that it had done its duty to preserving the Union by showing good faith in the promise to observe the Fugitive Slave Act.

Events on the national scene, however, left little opportunity for these actions to fester in the minds and consciences of northern Ohio Republicans. After the failure of peace compromise efforts and the withdrawal of Texas from the Union on February 1, the country seemed to be holding its breath waiting for the new president to take office. Clevelanders, however, were busily preparing for the visit of the president-elect—"Uncle Abe"—and his entourage. Lincoln's staff had planned a train trip from Springfield, Illinois, to Washington, D.C., which would take the presidential party through much of the Republican Midwest, with stopovers in some of the major cities which had given Lincoln their vote. Cleveland was one such city. Lincoln's train was to arrive from Pittsburgh at 4:00 P.M. Friday afternoon, February 15. According to the *Plain Dealer,* "trains from the South and West this morning brought crowds of people to witness the reception of Mr. LINCOLN. Flags are flying from the many liberty poles about the city. Numerous buildings are decorated with the stars and stripes and the streets look quite gay. The mud, however, is awful. The rain last night softened it up and some of the streets through which the procession will pass are a perfect mush."[11] The *Leader* noted with some pride that "Among the arrivals at the Angier, yesterday, were Messrs. Dutton, N.Y. Tribune; Howard, of N.Y. Times; Drake, of the Associated Press, Evans, N.Y. World, and Smith, of the Chicago Tribune, who are traveling with the Presidential party."[12]

People crowded the streets for hours awaiting the arrival of Lincoln. A *Leader* reporter wrote, "Several men and boys had gained the roof of the station-house. . . . Now and then a cry arose 'there they come,' and a simultaneous rush of the populace required all the efforts of the police and military to maintain their line unbroken." At length the report proved true, and a flag-adorned locomotive came into view. "Upon the stoppage of the train, Mr. Lincoln descended from his car, leaning upon the arms of two gentlemen, and bowing acknowledgements to the repeated cheers of the vast assemblage, proceeded to the carriage provided for him," continued the *Leader*'s account. A procession reminiscent of the Perry's Monument parade of the previous September provided an impressive escort. As enumerated in the *Leader,* it included wagons of the express companies, omnibuses of the Forest City Tool Co. and the Cuyahoga Steam Furnace Co., and a float containing a miniature full-rigged ship with a cannon on its deck. Thirty mounted young men formed an honor guard for Robert Todd Lincoln, son of the president-elect. Then came the Light Dragoons, the Cleveland Light Artillery Brigade, and the Cleveland Grays, followed by the carriages containing the presi-

Howard Melville Hanna represented his family by joining the navy in the Civil War, while his brother Marcus Alonzo remained behind to mind the family business and their widowed mother. Howard survived the war to join his brothers in forming the M. A. Hanna Company and engage in numerous other business and civic activities.

dential party and the various committees. The procession moved slowly down Euclid Street and reached the Weddell House at five o'clock.[13]

At the corner of Bank and Superior Streets west of Public Square, this hotel was the pride of the city, five stories high with more than 300 guest rooms, large ornate public parlors, and its famous recessed balcony supported by towering Doric columns. It was decked out in flags and red and blue bunting with a special platform erected out over the balcony from which the president-elect was to address the crowd. The presidential party took over one whole floor. Shortly after their arrival, an assemblage of distinguished Republican politicians, state legislators, and mayor George B. Senter made speeches of welcome, and Abraham Lincoln then briefly addressed the people below, thanking them for their welcome and admonishing them to support the Union. Commenting in the *Leader,* Edwin Cowles remarked, "Thus far Mr. Lincoln's addresses appear to us to be as appropriate as his previous silence had been judicious. Extempore remarks by a President elect, whose policy is yet to be exposed, are certainly delicate experiments."[14] This one was no exception.

The crowd's cheering was nearly ceaseless during and following Lincoln's address, after which the party withdrew to prepare for a splendid reception in one of the Weddell House's largest public parlors. (Among those who signed the hotel register that evening were John Hay, Lincoln's handsome young secretary who may have met his future father-in-law, Amasa Stone, among the city's leading businessmen in attendance with their wives. Clara Stone, whom Hay married more than a decade later, was probably not in attendance.)

The next morning the Cleveland Grays escorted the president-elect and his party to the Union Depot, where they entrained for Buffalo. Many local politicians rode along for short distances with the Lincoln party. Among them was Albert G. Riddle, lead defense lawyer for the Oberlin Rescuers and new congressman from Ohio's Nineteenth District. He left the train at Willoughby, where Lincoln spoke a few words to the crowd from the platform of the train and was given a cannon salute (which unfortunately happened to take off the arm of one of the firers).[15]

Lincoln's train did finally arrive in Washington, D.C., despite its slow progress and rumors of an assassination plot in Baltimore. Inauguration day, Monday morning, March 4, was dark, rainy, and cold. Congressman-elect Riddle was among those conducted to their places in the well-arranged Senate chamber at 11:00 A.M. "The President-elect, on the arm of the President, and the members-elect of his Cabinet, entered a little past twelve," wrote Riddle. "I had seen and heard Mr. Buchanan at the rival Democratic conventions at Erie, September 10, 1849, and then rather admired him, Whig as I was. He was old now, with a sad, worn, withered, white face, stouter and seemingly shorter, with his well developed head in its fixed inclination to the left shoulder. He had an air of resolve and bore

A member of the Lincoln entourage on the president-elect's stopover in Cleveland was young John Milton Hay, Lincoln's private secretary. He would return to the city after the Civil War to marry Clara Stone and occupy a mansion on Euclid Avenue. The chief fruit of his residence was the anonymously authored *The Bread-Winners,* perhaps the most noteworthy novel ever set in Cleveland.

There were five Rockefeller siblings living in the house young John D. had built for them on Cheshire Street on the eve of the Civil War. Pictured (left to right) are John, Mary Ann, Lucy, William, and Frank. It was Frank who lied about his age to join the 7th Volunteer Infantry, the first regiment to leave Cleveland.

himself well."[16] After witnessing the swearing-in of vice president Hannibal Hamlin, the assemblage moved outdoors for the inauguration of Abraham Lincoln.

"In the accident of places on the broad extemporized platform (which extended out over the wide steps leading up to the rotunda in front of the Capitol), I was landed within four or five feet of Mr. Lincoln when he delivered his memorable and most fortunate address," continued Congressman Riddle. "Never was there a more persuasive speaker. His quaint logic and taking, unaccustomed ways were absolutely irresistible. His vocabulary was limited, he used mainly the simple words that one learns in childhood, which are always the most serviceable."[17] Lincoln, indeed, ended his inaugural address with simple language and a haunting metaphor of the harp. "I am loth to close," he said, addressing the seceding states. "We are not enemies, but friends. We must not be enemies. Though passion may have been strained, it must not break our bonds of affection. The mystic chords of memory, stretching from every battle-field, and patriot grave, to every living heart and hearthstone, all over this broad land, will yet swell the chorus of the Union, when again touched, as surely they will be, by the better angels of our nature." President Lincoln then placed his tall, black stovepipe hat firmly on his head and, towering over the dark-suited men who swarmed around him, left the platform to take an open carriage down Pennsylvania Avenue to the White House. The inaugural address was immediately telegraphed to the Cleveland pressrooms of the *Herald,* the *Plain Dealer,* and the *Leader,* which in the evening and morning editions praised the speech.

Tension, however, continued to build throughout March and into April as the clamor for secession continued in the upper tier of Southern states and as Federal buildings, arsenals, and forts were taken over by the new Confederacy. Only two major forts remained in Federal possession: Fort Pickens at Pensacola Harbor in Florida and Fort Sumter at the mouth of the harbor of Charleston, South Carolina. Lincoln, after much internal wrangling, decided to reinforce both forts secretly. The secret, however, leaked out, and Confederate forces under Gen. Pierre G. T. Beauregard began firing on Fort Sumter.

On that Friday morning, April 12, Jacob D. Cox, state senator from Warren, was in the Ohio Senate chamber trying, as he recalled, to go on with business in the ordinary routine but with a sense of anxiety and strain that was caused by the troubled condition of national affairs. "But there was no heart in it, and the morning hour lagged," he wrote. "Suddenly a senator came in from the lobby in an excited way and, catching the chairman's eye, exclaimed, 'Mr. President, the telegraph announces that the secessionists are bombarding Fort Sumter!' There was a solemn and painful hush, but it was broken in a moment by a woman's shrill voice from the spectators' seats, crying, 'Glory to God!'"[18] Was there a secessionist in the chamber? No, it was the voice of Abby Kelly Foster, famous Massachusetts feminist and abolitionist lecturer, who had been touring Ohio and was convinced that only war could wipe out the sin of slavery. (Tradition would have it that her outcry was the first feminine voice ever raised in the Ohio legislature.) Her sentiments were echoed by many, including Ohio state senator James Garfield, the thirty-year-old principal of the Western Reserve Eclectic Institute (later Hiram College), who predicted in a letter from Columbus to his Hiram colleague J. H. Rhodes on April 13 that "the war will soon assume the shape of Slavery & Freedom[.] The world will so understand it—& I believe the final outcome will redound to the good of humanity."[19]

The telegraph lines that Cleveland's Jeptha Wade only a few years before had consolidated into the new Western Union company brought instantaneous news dispatches from individual correspondents as well as hourly reports by the new Associated Press. "By our telegraphic dispatches," said the *Leader*, "it will be seen that the ball has been opened and the dance of death has begun." Headlines screamed

WAR BEGUN!
Gen. Beaureguard demands the surrender of Fort Sumter!
ANDERSON REFUSES.
THE BATTERIES OPEN FIRE.
THE ATTACK COMMENCED YESTERDAY MORNING.
REPORTED BREACHES IN FORT SUMTER![20]

The *Plain Dealer* noted that "the City of Charleston is now bristling with bayonets, and the Harbor blazing with rockets and booming with big guns."[21] Maj. Robert Anderson and his small garrison of only eighty men were forced to surrender for

Rebecca Rouse was well qualified to assume leadership in the efforts of Cleveland women to aid Northern troops in the Civil War. Drawing on her experiences with such causes as the Cleveland Ladies Temperance Union and the Protestant Orphan Asylum, she quickly organized a Ladies' (later the Northern Ohio Soldiers') Aid Society. Almost immediately its members began combing the city to collect blankets for the recruits pouring into Camp Taylor.

lack of supplies and munitions. Edwin Cowles soberly mused from his editor's chair, "We are not unmindful of the horrors of civil war. It is the most horrible of all forms in which 'grim visaged war' comes upon the earth. Brother and friend fighting against brother and friend; one portion of our country arrayed against another; acquaintances and partners drawn up in battle against each other, their hands reeking with each other's blood—these are pictures which we would to God we were never compelled to look upon. But no alternative is left us now."[22] That day Lincoln called for 75,000 three-month volunteers to come to Washington to protect the capital city.

On the same day that the *Leader* published Lincoln's call for volunteers, Edwin Cowles added his own call: "Men of Ohio! the Flag of our Country . . . has been torn down from its standard, and left to trail in the dust beneath the banner of a rebellious host! Shall it remain there? . . . Ohio must be in the van of the battle."[23] There followed almost daily notices of new companies forming and recruiters coming into town. One appeared on April 18: "A new company of Infantry under the name of 'Company A.' is being enrolled among the Germans." On the same day Edward Kinsman advertised, "I propose to raise a company of one hundred men, (the officers to be elected by the Company), to be uniformed with red flannel shirts, black pants and slouched hats, and to be called the 'Garibaldians.'" Applicants were instructed to appear at "the Brigade Headquarters, Lyman's Block."[24] A few days later: "Good musicians are wanted for volunteer service. They should report April 29 at Camp Taylor, state fair grounds. Regular army wages will be paid. Come one, come all!"[25] The *Leader* noted that "military movement in the city is very intense, companies being formed one after another. Some companies are already on their way to active service, others will soon follow."[26] A temporary military camp was set up on the Cuyahoga County Agricultural Society Fairgrounds along Kinsman Avenue on the southeast side. The new enlistees had to build their own barracks and erect their own tents. New recruits came in by train from Painesville, Ashtabula, Sandusky, and Mansfield. Crowds gathered daily at the fairgrounds to watch the recruits drill, and superintendent of schools Andrew Freese complained that students were playing hooky to join those crowds.

Not every young man, however, rushed out to enlist. Marcus Alonzo Hanna had joined his father's commission house business, Hanna, Garretson & Company, working on the company's freight steamers as well as in the warehouse on Merwin Street. Hanna continued to enjoy life—sports, the races, dances, and people—and had not applied himself to the business until his father, Dr. Leonard Hanna, fell ill and was dying. He then took over his father's share of the partnership and the work. During the enlistment furor, Marcus (age twenty-three) and his brother Howard Melville (age twenty-one) talked it over and agreed that Mar-

The First Presbyterian Church has been a Public Square landmark since 1833. The original building was replaced in 1855 by the familiar Romanesque Revival structure popularly known as the Old Stone Church. It played an active role on the Civil War home front, from serving as a depot for the spoils of the "blanket raid" for local recruits to providing a temporary shelter for the care of Southern refugees.

cus would have to stay home and take care of his mother's interest in the business while Howard enlisted in the navy.

Marcus's former classmate at Central High School, John D. Rockefeller, was in a similar bind; his commission house had just begun to prosper and he had taken over the support of his mother and sister. "I wanted to go in the army and do my part," he later explained. "But it was simply out of the question. There was no one to take my place. We were in a new business, and if I had not stayed it might have stopped—and with so many dependent on it."[27] His younger brother Frank, however, did enlist in the 7th Ohio Volunteer Infantry Regiment. Although he was only sixteen, he allegedly chalked the number "18" on the sole of each of his boots. When the recruiting sergeant asked how old he was, he blithely said, "I'm over eighteen, sir!"[28] Brother John provided him with clothes, money, and rifle and reportedly was similarly generous toward other enlistees, their families, and local war relief funds. According to Capt. Levi Scofield, Rockefeller one morning dispensed ten dollars to each of thirty recruits the captain had led to his office on River Street.

Cleveland's young women also mobilized five days after Lincoln's call for volunteers. On Friday, April 19, the *Herald* published a notice addressed to "The patriotic ladies of Cleveland, anxious and ready to take their full share in the exertions and privations, if need be, imposed by the public perils," inviting them to attend a meeting at Chapin's Hall on the corner of Euclid and Public Square on Saturday, April 20, at three o'clock. The following afternoon Euclid Avenue

Headquarters for the Soldiers' Aid Society of Northern Ohio was this rented storefront at 95 Bank (West 6th) Street. Here clothing, medical supplies, and food were received from all over northern Ohio by the female staff and distributed to soldiers in camps and the field. "Every town within shipping distance of Cleveland sent again and again its offering," wrote secretary Mary Clark Brayton. The local society was affiliated with the quasi-official U.S. Sanitary Commission.

was crowded with carriages carrying ladies, matrons, and young girls; and lines of women wearing bonnets and long coats in muted colors streamed toward the three-story brownstone building that was Chapin's Hall. They climbed the stairways to the third floor, where they emerged into a grand, gas-lit auditorium containing 1,200 upholstered seats. When the hall filled, the noise level dropped as a short, gray-haired woman strode with serious purpose to the podium. Mrs. Benjamin (Rebecca) Rouse was a familiar figure to many of the ladies in the audience who had worked with the Protestant Orphanage Society, the Cleveland Ladies Temperance Union, or the Protestant Sunday schools. She wasted no time in getting to the purpose of the meeting, which was to organize the women of Cleveland to raise funds and collect supplies for volunteers and their families. After electing officers and pledging twenty-five cents a month as members of the new Ladies' Aid Society (soon to be called the Soldiers' Aid Society of Northern Ohio), the women divided up into ward visiting committees to see to the needs of the families of soldiers.

But even before visiting could begin, an emergency arose that would immediately expand the work of the society. Word came to Rebecca Rouse that a thousand recruits were expected at the temporary military camp on Kinsman and that there were no blankets. She immediately hired eight hacks and asked sixteen young ladies to volunteer to collect blankets. One of the young volunteers was Caroline Younglove, who later recalled the "blanket raid." According to her account, she took one of the carriages and drove up and down the streets of the West Side accompanied by Flora Payne, daughter of attorney Henry B. Payne. "We stopped at every house, big and little, rich or poor, and I wish you could have seen the piles of beautiful blankets and quilts and comfortables given to us," she wrote. "Everyone gave us all that they could spare, and of their best, and our carriage was filled over and over again. People would hear that we were coming, and I can remember how the things were piled on the sidewalk, so that as we came past we had only to gather them up. For two days we drove up one street and down another, until every volunteer was amply provided for."[29]

The initial yield of the "blanket raid" was stacked in the parlors of the First Presbyterian (Old Stone) Church on Public Square. As Mary Clark Brayton recalled, there were stacks of "delicate rose blankets, chintz quilts, thick counterpanes, and by nightfall seven hundred and twenty-nine blankets were carried into camp. Next morning the work was resumed, and before another night every volunteer at Camp Taylor had been provided for."[30]

While the "blanket raid" was going on, other women noted a raggedy troop of new recruits marching to fife and drum down Superior Street, wearing only their worn work clothes (apparently assuming that as soon as they arrived at camp they would be furnished with uniforms, which was not to be the case). The ladies took charge and requisitioned "a quantity of Army flannel." Professional tailors contributed patterns and the services of their cutters. Rooms in the Young Men's Christian Association (Seneca, or West 3rd, and Superior) were used as a depot, and from there the materials were distributed. "The Grover & Baker and Wheeler & Wilson sewing machine rooms were thrown open and were soon crowded with industrious dames, some cutting, some basting, and others guiding the fast-flying machines," Brayton wrote. "In two days one thousand army shirts were cut, given out, finished and returned to camp."[31]

Throughout the rest of April and May and into early June, committees of the Ladies' Aid Society were busied in gathering old clothing, blankets, and hospital stores for the regiments that continued to assemble at Camp Taylor, rushing to fill President Lincoln's call to arms. The scene was chaotic, like the rest of the mobilization effort around the country. There was no single source of information as to what was, or would be, needed, so some mistakes, large and small, were made—such as the "havelock" craze. Designed by Sir James Havelock to keep British troops in the North African desert cool, the havelock was a hat cover of light-colored linen with flaps that stretched down to the shoulders from ear to ear. The ladies got word from "the East" that these "ugly things" were necessary for field service, so they set to work. "For weeks much superfluous enthusiasm was worked into these grotesque headpieces," wrote Mary Brayton. "The stiff linen was cut by many aching fingers and given out in parcels to ladies who would return the finished articles in a fabulously short time. Thus an ample supply was soon furnished to each Northern Ohio regiment."[32] While received with much gratitude and enthusiasm, the "grotesque" hat covers were soon discarded. It seems they prevented air circulation around the head, making the soldier hotter rather than cooler. Word filtered back to the ladies, and all havelock manufacture stopped.

Between June and July the Soldiers' Aid Society, as it was now known, rented a storefront at 95 Bank (West 6th) Street to serve as a distribution center. And although work slowed as Camp Taylor emptied, word continued to come back from various officers of particular needs that were quickly filled. During the hectic and heady bustle of those first six weeks, most people hoped, and some believed, that something would happen in July, and it would all be over. None could foresee the gigantic mobilization effort ahead and the long, arduous work over the years to come.

Meanwhile, in Washington, D.C., Albert Riddle watched the activity with great anticipation. He visited with Ohio regiments as they moved into forts around Washington. He gossiped with other congressmen about when the army would move or whether Southern troops would attempt to attack Washington. Troops were camped all over town, including in the Capitol Rotunda and the House of Representatives chamber. The city was awash in military uniforms, from the scarlet pantaloons and white cravats of the Zouaves to the dark blue of the Union Army.

By mid-July there were rumors all over town of an impending battle on the road to Richmond. Albert Riddle was mindful of his promise to the company of Cleveland Grays. "I was under promise to our Grays, that if a battle was fought within reach of Washington I would join them if possible, and share their fortunes on the field," he wrote. He obtained a pass from Gen. Winfield Scott, "a strong carriage, a pair of stout horses, a good driver, a hamper of lunch, and four of the largest navy revolvers. . . . I also had my Remingtons."[33] Along with three colleagues he set off on Sunday morning, July 21, and by the late afternoon had reached Centerville on the Warrenton Turnpike to Richmond.

By the time Riddle and his party arrived, they could hear artillery firing. It was around 4:30 in the afternoon when they began to meet up with stragglers back from the battle who first told them the Rebels were retreating. Riddle and his companions pushed on until they could see Union forces, apparently retreating toward them in order. When a Rebel shell blew up a Union munitions wagon, the ranks broke and the troops ran in panic, followed by the wagons of other civilian spectators. Riddle was forced to turn with the tide.

Brig. Gen. Irvin McDowell had been ordered by Lincoln to march to prevent Jefferson Davis and the new Confederate government from convening in Richmond, their new capital. McDowell's army, assembled from 35,000 raw recruits who surrounded Washington, then marched toward Richmond, reaching Centerville (twenty-six miles south of Washington) in two days. There McDowell set up headquarters and began reconnoitering the Southern defenses thrown up in the woods and hills south of a muddy creek, Bull Run, protecting the vital railroad junction of Manassas. At 2:00 A.M. Sunday, McDowell started his army toward the Confederate forces. The battle ensued. At one time, around noon, the Confederates were being pushed back, but reinforcements forced the retreat of a portion of McDowell's line, and by 4:00 P.M. Union forces were in full but orderly retreat. The spectators' carriages and wagons, however, rushing back toward Washington, had jammed the Warrenton Turnpike, turning the Union retreat into a surging tide of blue rushing pell-mell toward the Northern capital.

Congressman Riddle described the scene in a letter to his wife a day later. "It seemed as if the very devil of panic and cowardice seized every mortal soldier, officer, citizen, and teamster," he wrote. "No officer tried to rally the soldiers or do anything except to spring and run toward Centerville. There never was anything like it for a causeless, sheer, absolute, absurd panic on this miserable earth before. Off they went, one and all, off down the highway, over across the fields towards

After marching in the parade welcoming president-elect Lincoln to the city, the Cleveland Grays became the first military unit of Clevelanders to leave for the front in the Civil War. They were organized in 1837 as an independent volunteer militia company. According to congressman Albert G. Riddle, an eyewitness, the Grays were the first on the field and the last to leave in the first Battle of Bull Run.

the woods, anywhere, everywhere, to escape." Despite their sturdy horses and carriages, Riddle's party was outdistanced by the retreating Union soldiers, who left a disorderly trail of discarded blankets, knapsacks, canteens, muskets, and cartridge boxes in their wake. "We called to them, tried to tell them there was no danger, called them to stop, implored them to stand," continued Riddle. "We called them cowards, denounced them in most offensive terms, put out our heavy revolvers, and threatened to shoot them, but all in vain. A cruel, crazy, mad, helpless panic possessed them, and was communicated to everybody about, in front and rear." Crazed with the heat and exhaustion, the fugitives were oblivious to any appeals or threats. Only the blocked roads in the rear of the Union positions slowed them down, allowing Riddle to catch up with them. "As we passed, the poor, demented, exhausted wretches, who could not climb into the high, close baggage-wagons, made frantic efforts to get into and onto our carriage. . . . At first they loaded us down to a standstill. We had to be rough with them and thrust them out and off, and Brown and I guarded the doors with pistols. One poor devil did get in, and we lugged the pitiful coward a mile or two. He wore major's straps, was hatless, and had thrown away his sword; finally I opened the door and he tumbled—or was tumbled out."[34]

Portions of Riddle's letter were published in the *Leader*. Two days later, July 19, 1861, George Benedict wrote an editorial in the *Herald* charging Riddle with cowardice and lack of patriotism. Whether merited or not, the charges stuck and later would cost Riddle his seat in Congress. He stayed on in Washington, writing articles and books about the war. To his credit, he wrote another letter to the *Leader* praising the 1st Ohio Volunteer Infantry Regiment and the Cleveland Grays. "The 1st Ohio that covered the retreat in their part of the field, came off in perfect order," he wrote. "And our own gallant Grays, as they were the first in, so they were the last out of the battle."[35]

The day after the humiliating defeat at Bull Run, President Lincoln signed a bill into law authorizing the three-year enlistment of 300,000 men. Grim determination supplanted patriotic bravado. It was clear now that this would not be a short war.

The Hard Road to Freedom

JAMES GARFIELD HAD NO DOUBT that this war was to be a war for freedom and that it would take more than a year of fighting and many bitter defeats before freedom would become an official and recognized goal of the war. In Washington, Congress made it emphatically clear that emancipation was not initially to be a war aim. On July 22, the day after the humiliating defeat at Bull Run, the following resolution was passed by the House of Representatives: "That the present deplorable civil war has been forced upon the country by the disunionists of the Southern States, now in arms against the constitutional Government, and in arms around the Capital; that in this national emergency Congress, banishing all feelings of mere passion or resentment, will recollect only its duty to the whole country; that this war is not waged on their part in any spirit of oppression, or for any purpose of conquest or subjugation, or purpose of overthrowing or interfering with the rights of established institutions of those States, but to defend and maintain the supremacy of the Constitution and to preserve the Union."

This declaration, known as the Crittenden Resolution, after its sponsor, Representative John J. Crittenden of the border state of Kentucky, passed the House with only two "nay" votes, one of which was cast by Albert G. Riddle from northeast Ohio's Western Reserve. After casting his vote, Riddle recalled, he walked out of the chamber in disgust. His colleagues told him to go back in and change his vote. He retorted furiously, "In God's name, gentlemen, what do you mean? Not a man of you believes that slavery is eternal. Not one is stupid enough, *notwithstanding his vote,* to believe that it can be abolished by convention. You all believe that it is to go out, when it does go, through convulsion, fire, and blood. That convulsion is upon us. The man is a delirious ass who does not see and realize this. For me I mean to make a conquest of it; to beat it to extinction under the iron hoofs of our war horses."[1]

Prior to his election to Congress in 1860, Albert Gallatin Riddle had been a member of the defense team in the trial of the Oberlin slave rescuers. He was one of only two congressmen to vote against the Crittenden Resolution, which declared that the Civil War was being fought solely to preserve the Union and not to interfere with the institution of slavery. Though events proved him right, he failed to win renomination for a second term.

What had begun as a war to preserve the Union would indeed, as foreseen by Riddle, become over time a war to end slavery. It was the very length of the conflict that led to the gradual evolution of Northern war aims. Bull Run was only the first of dozens of battles that would alternately raise and lower each side's hopes of victory. While northern Ohioans could keep up with the fortunes of war through the accounts printed in their local newspapers, many got much more vivid and personal accounts of the boredom of camp life, as well as the confusion of battle, from the letters of their brothers and sons in the Union Army.

With his call for 300,000 volunteers, President Lincoln named George B. McClellan, brigadier general of Ohio Volunteer Infantry, to take charge of forming a fighting army on the national level. Preparations began to wage a full-scale war. In Cleveland enlistments picked up pace in August and September, as recruiting notices for new companies or regiments seemed, once again, to appear almost daily. Camp Taylor was reactivated, and four new camps around town (two more on the East Side and two on the West) were authorized to receive the trainloads of recruits coming in from the towns and villages of northeast Ohio.

Frank Rieley, a Brooklyn Township boy, barely eighteen, enlisted in the 3rd Ohio Volunteer Cavalry in September 1861. While living with his parents, five brothers, and a sister, he had worked as a plasterer with his father, Hugh. He would have joined up earlier, but his parents, and particularly his mother, objected. Frank, determined to enlist, set out walking toward Columbus, beyond the reach of his parents. About halfway there, in the town of Shelby, just north of Mansfield, he fell in with some fellows that were being recruited to join a new cavalry regiment. The recruits were taken north to Monroeville, where they joined others in the newly formed regiment at Camp Worcester, "about fifteen miles south of Sandusky," according to Frank. Meanwhile, his mother and father were frantic. They drove to all the temporary training camps in Cleveland to search in vain for their son or for word of him. Finally, Margaret Rieley received a letter from her son in Monroeville, informing her of his travels and assuring her that he was "well fed with pork, beans, potatoes, beef, bread and butter and plenty of coffee" and "well satisfied" with his decision.[2]

"You may well wonder that I should leave a situation where I could make an easy living and enlist as a soldier, but believe me that I did not want to do it because I hated work, but I did it because it was my duty to do it, and I think it is the duty of at least one out of each family to go and fight for his country," explained Frank. He didn't think he could hold his head up among his fellow citizens if it were said that such a large family as his could send none to its country's defense. "You may say that I owe my parents more than I owe the Country, but I consider that I am doing a duty that they will some day be thankful for. If I get safely through this war as I hope I shall, it will help me along a little and people will know that I have grit in me." Rieley closed with a request that his brother John go to a bookstore to get him some treatises on calvary tactics.[3]

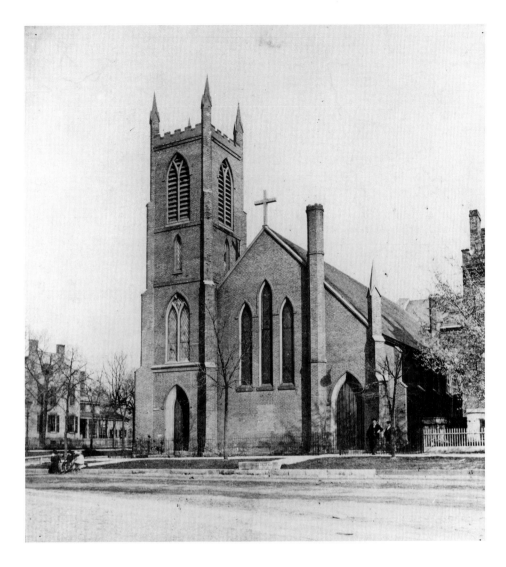

Located at Huron and Erie (East 9th) Streets, Grace Episcopal Church was recognized along with Trinity as one of the denomination's local "high-church" parishes. Alexander Varian Jr., son of the founding rector, was an early Northern volunteer in the Civil War.

While Margaret and Hugh Rieley were searching the camps in Cleveland for their son, another young Clevelander, Alexander Varian Jr., succumbed to the increased pace of recruiting and was on the train to Camp Corwin outside of Dayton to join the 1st Ohio Volunteer Infantry Regiment. He came from an equally large family of brothers and sisters, his father being the first rector of Grace Episcopal Church at Huron and Erie (East 9th) streets. Young Alex wrote to his father almost immediately upon arriving at Camp Corwin: "Here I am safe and sound after a very fatiguing day. . . . I expect to be sworn in this afternoon & get my clothes. So far I am none the worse for camp life. I am writing in my tent with my carpet sack for a desk."[4]

Three days later he wrote his sister, Laura, that he had been issued a uniform consisting of two gray woolen shirts and drawers, two pairs of white woolen socks, and a pair of dark blue pants with blouse and cap to match. "They all fitted very well except the pants which were . . . made for a chap considerably larger than myself," he wrote, "but I took them down to the river & shrunk them up

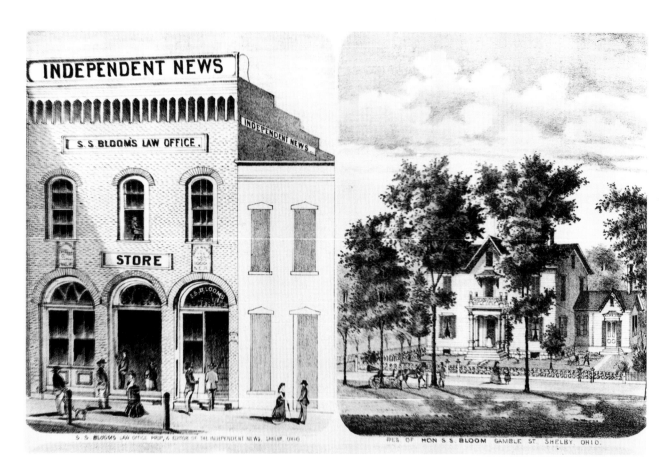

Cleveland was the hub for scores of northern Ohio towns such as Shelby, where Frank Rieley decided to enlist in the cavalry rather than continue on to Columbus. Later, as his company again passed through Shelby on its way south, they were given a "first-rate" ball by the townspeople.

to quite a respectable size." He also confessed to a bout with "'Diarrhea' & vomiting" though he was much improved thanks to "some powders" prescribed by a doctor and the ministrations of a "Hospital Stewart" from Painesville known as "Live Yankee." "He enlisted in Cleveland & when asked his name said 'Live Yankee' & has gone by that name ever since," explained Varian. "He is great on Union speeches and affords amusement for the whole regiment." Though Varian felt well enough to return to duty, Live Yankee wouldn't hear of it, "so I have concluded to keep sick a little longer, but I think I shall be all right by tomorrow night. It is nothing but what every man in the Reg'm't has had to go through."[5]

As he promised Laura, Varian wrote to his younger sister Hettie with a description of his "rations," which consisted of "1 cup of what the cook calls, *coffee*," a two-inch slice of "Baker's bread," a concoction of "oats & beans & barley corns," boiled potatoes, and a "hunk" of salted or fresh meat. "These are all taken in your hands, as Uncle Sam has not given us plates, knives or forks as yet," commented Varian. "The 'nack' of it is to eat your 'grub' without getting it in the dirt or burning your fingers." Evenings were given over to sacred music, as Varian accompanied a friend named Farwell on his flute. "He is a very good bass singer and we have our tent crowded every night."[6]

In September, while Alex Varian and Frank Rieley were adjusting to camp life,

Oliver Hazard Payne, age twenty-two, returned to Yale for the fall semester with grim determination to continue his college studies. As he wrote his older brother, Nathan, on October 3, "I am not wholly contented here and had I my own way, to be candid, would leave tomorrow and enlist, be it nothing more than as a high private—knowing Fathers wishes & desires were so strong for me remaining at my studies, I had hoped when I once returned that I might be so engaged as to forget myself in my books."[7] His father, Henry B. Payne, was a very successful Cleveland lawyer, businessman, and politician. An organizer and former president of the Cleveland, Columbus & Cincinnati Railroad, he campaigned nationally for Stephen A. Douglas in 1860. He was also very ambitious for his sons. He had sent Oliver to Yale not only for a college education but to make contacts that would promote his career in business or law when he returned to Cleveland.

Oliver had shown signs of war fever as early as April 1861 when he had written his mother to describe the passage of a Massachusetts regiment through New Haven on its way to Washington: "From the time they first made their appearance till they left, the air rung with shouts, bayonets gleamed aloft; and as far as you could see in any direction fair hands waved snowy kerchiefs." Oliver confessed his own temptation to join the next regiment to be raised if there were no parental objections, "as I am strong, healthy and in every way capable to endure the hardships attendant upon it."[8] His father did indeed reply with strong objections.

Clevelanders provided a solid nucleus of the First Ohio Light Artillery Regiment, which absorbed the militia unit known as the Cleveland Light Artillery. Batteries from this regiment served in both eastern and western theaters of the Civil War. It sustained a total of nearly 500 casualties.

Left: Against his father's wishes that he continue his studies at Yale, Oliver Hazard Payne left college to enlist in an Illinois regiment. Later he transferred to a newly organized Cleveland regiment, becoming colonel of the 124th Ohio Volunteer Infantry. Wounded at Chickamauga, he left the army after the Atlanta campaign and eventually became treasurer of the Standard Oil Company.

Right: Initially opposed to his son Oliver's enlistment, Cleveland lawyer and businessman Henry B. Payne would have preferred that young Payne first complete his Yale education. His parental feelings may have been soothed to some extent when Oliver later sent him five gallons of aged whisky from the field in Kentucky. A Douglas Democrat, the elder Payne was later elected to the U.S. House of Representatives, where he was named to the Electoral Commission charged with settling the disputed 1876 presidential election.

Oliver would be throwing away his future; he should stay and take his degree and then perhaps, if the war was still on, he could obtain a commission. Oliver acquiesced, though as he later wrote his brother Nathan, he was no longer happy at Yale.

Far from resigning himself to settling back into his studies, Oliver was working hard to find a position in the army that would suit his father's ambitions and allay his fears about Oliver's future. He wrote to Nathan laying out a plan he had to enlist in Illinois with a college chum who happened to be the son of a former governor of that state. His friend had used his connections to secure an appointment as major with the promise of a captaincy or lieutenancy for young Payne. Oliver rationalized that "I have about made up my mind to go into business after graduating—so that at the end of two years I would throw up my books even if I remained here." Making influential contacts in the West and "winning some little distinction" in the war would do more to advance a future business career than two more years at Yale.[9]

When next heard from, Oliver was in Illinois helping to recruit a regiment known as "Yates' Sharpshooters," named for the governor of Illinois. He and his college friend, Maj. Fred Matteson, set up shop in Joliet, Illinois. (Oliver's own commission was pending on the formation of the regiment.) "We arrived here yesterday," he wrote his father, "having opened our office, paraded hand Bills pretty extensively—used a good deal of printers ink & have set to work with energy bound to raise a company or nearly one in about a week—we have so far met with good success, having already picked up four men."[10] By November the regiment was all but filled and, after an irritating wait for slow contractors to finish the barracks and headquarters buildings at Camp Butler in Springfield, he and the men moved into their winter barracks.

Payne settled into camp life, drilling the men and, as adjutant, taking care of much of the regimental paperwork. He was often too tired to sleep well but had adjusted wonderfully well to army food after overcoming an initial fastidiousness. In a letter home to Nathan, he advised his brother to "throw up the Coal business" and try to procure some government contracts, as "there is any amount of money to be made in it."[11]

Frank Rieley, too, was settling into camp life. "Dear Mother and Friends," he wrote in mid-October, "our time is nearly all taken up in drilling and [we] have very little time to spare. We have received our caps, shirts, drawers and boots and expect to receive the rest of our uniforms next week."[12] Later letters informed the folks of the arrival of uniforms, warm overcoats, and horses. "It is getting pretty cold here and we are all anxious to be moving further south," he wrote on December 4. Sure enough, in January Frank's regiment rode back to Shelby. "On the road from Monroeville to Shelby we were furnished all the pies, cakes, apples, etc. we could eat and carry," he recounted. After being given a "first-rate" ball at Shelby, Rieley's company then entrained for Camp Dennison near Cincinnati. "It is hilly and we could see into Kentucky on clear days," he reported.[13] There the men were finally issued their sabers, and Frank was promoted to corporal.

Clevelander Morris I. Holly, a twenty-two-year-old Superior Street grocery clerk, joined the 7th Ohio Volunteer Infantry and was also sent to Camp Dennison for more training before being marched onto railroad cars and moved to Washington, D.C. Writing home to his sister Elizabeth (Lizzie) Hunter of Miami Street, he described the enthusiastic citizen support that the soldiers met with all

One of some score of regiments raised largely in Cleveland was the 107th Ohio Volunteer Infantry, which was organized and trained at Camp Taylor on Woodland Avenue. Filled to a large extent by German Americans, the unit saw action in the major engagements of Fredericksburg, Chancellorsville, and Gettysburg. They served from 1862 to the end of the war, losing 133 men to enemy action or disease.

Largest of Cleveland's seven Civil War camp sites was Camp Cleveland, located in what was then called Cleveland Heights and is now known as Tremont. Some 15,000 officers and men trained in the 35-acre site, which included this hospital. Another of the camp's sights was the "Secesh Cannon," captured in western Virginia by the Cleveland Light Artillery and fired off to salute Union victories.

along the route, the kind of patriotism that Oliver H. Payne had witnessed in New Haven. "We were well received at the station along the road. [T]he citizens bring us water and provisions and with a good bye and a god-bless you we again moved on." He wrote of how, late one evening, he and his comrades were stopped by the sight of a seventy-year-old woman standing on a grassy knoll and dramatically outlined against a gorgeous sunset. "Here she stood like a godest [*sic*] of liberty with that banner which we ackno[w]ledge gently thrown around her form[,] her wright arm raised aloft—her eyes gently turned towards heaven and as we stoped she addressed us as follows. 'Yong men and soldiers[.] [M]ay god give you the power as I know you have the courage to protect this flag (Gently laying her hand on the stars and strips) and may the time [soon] come when it shall again wave in peace and power throughout the whole nation.'"[14] (This image of a woman wrapped in the Stars and Stripes with her hand upraised was very popular throughout the war and appeared on letterheads, in verse, and in song. The most famous was John Greenleaf Whittier's poem, "Barbara Frietchie," who, facing the invading troops of Stonewall Jackson in Frederick, Maryland, raised the Stars and Stripes: "Shoot, if you must, this old gray head, / But spare your country's flag," she said.)

Cuyahoga County furnished a total of 10,000 soldiers for the Union effort throughout the war's duration. First to march were the Cleveland Grays, who saw action in the war's first major battle at Bull Run. Another Cleveland militia unit, the Cleveland Light Artillery, saw early action in western Virginia and brought back a captured Confederate field piece. Known locally as the "Secesh Cannon," it was prominently displayed at Camp Cleveland on the West Side, where it was fired to salute the departure of troops and the arrival of news of Union victories.

Oberlin, considered by many to be "the town that started the Civil War" with its Oberlin-Wellington Rescue, didn't shirk its duty when the firing started. Several hundred men from both town and college responded to Lincoln's first call for

The Battle-Cry of Freedom.

Published by Chas. Magnus, 12 Frankfort St. New York.

Yes, we'll rally round the Flag, boys, we'll rally once again,
  Shouting the battle-cry of Freedom ;
We will rally from the hill-side, we'll gather from the plain,
  Shouting the battle-cry of Freedom !
            CHORUS.
    The Union for ever ! hurrah ! boys, hurrah !
      Down with the Traitor up with the Star !
    While we rally round the Flag, boys, rally once again
      Shouting the battle-cry of Freedom !

We are springing to the call of our Brothers gone before,
  Shouting the battle-cry of Freedom !
And we'll fill the vacant ranks with a million Freemen more,
  Shouting the battle-cry of Freedom !
      Chorus : The Union for ever ! &c.

We will welcome to our numbers the boys all true and brave,
  Shouting the battle cry of Freedom !
And although he may be poor he shall never be a Slave
  Shouting the battle-cry of Freedom !
      Chorus : The Union for ever ! &c.

So, we're springing to the call from the East and from
                                    the West,
  Shouting the battle-cry of Freedom !
And we'll hurl the Rebel crew from the land we love the best,
  Shouting the battle-cry of Freedom !
      Chorus : The Union for ever ! &c.

Ten illustrated Songs on Notepaper, mailed to any Address on
receipt of 50 cts. Published by Chas. Magnus, 12 Frankfort St., N. Y.

Familiar icons during the Civil War were those of Miss Liberty and the American flag. They were often paired, as in this broadside illustration for George F. Root's popular war song, "The Battle-Cry of Freedom." Patriotic Northern women sometimes acted these images out in living tableaus, such as that witnessed by Cleveland recruit Morris Holly.

volunteers after Fort Sumter. The college's faculty rescinded a regulation barring students from joining military companies, and more than 750 Oberlin alumni and students served in Ohio units during the war, six gaining the rank of general. At least half a dozen of the Oberlin rescuers themselves saw service in the conflict they allegedly had helped to ignite.

Ohio on the whole provided more than 300,000 troops to the Federal forces, a total exceeded only by the more populous states of New York and Pennsylvania. Asked to provide thirteen regiments as the state's quota after Fort Sumter, Ohio governor William Dennison informed Secretary of War Simon Cameron that he could not stop short of twenty. "The lion in us is thoroughly aroused," he wrote. In the proportion of its population to serve, Ohio was said to have led all the Northern states. Cleveland and the Western Reserve certainly did their share in this respect. The only recruitment area in which Ohio could be said to have lagged was in the enlistment of African American troops. Still barred by law from serving in the state militia, black Ohioans' efforts to enlist in what they saw as a struggle against slavery were initially rebuffed by state officials.

More than twenty of Ohio's 230 regiments were recruited in Cleveland and the surrounding area. First came the 7th Ohio Volunteer Infantry, the regiment of Morris Holly and Frank Rockefeller. The 23rd OVI was distinguished by the presence of two future presidents, Rutherford B. Hayes and William McKinley. Cleveland Germans dominated the 107th OVI, which fought in the Fredericksburg, Chancellorsville, and Gettysburg campaigns. Among those units campaigning in the Western theater was the 103rd OVI, which saw action at Knoxville and Atlanta. And finally, it was the 6th Ohio Volunteer Cavalry that opened the final battle of the war at Appomattox Court House.

Not all Buckeyes served in Ohio regiments, and Oliver Hazard Payne soon regretted his rash decision to enlist in Illinois. He made an unsuccessful effort to secure a commission in the 103rd OVI, "it being composed of Clevelanders would have made it quite pleasant, & perhaps in the End profitable to have been associated with them," as he wrote his brother Nathan.[15] Finally he succeeded in getting an appointment as lieutenant colonel in the 124th OVI, which was organized in Cleveland in the fall of 1862.

Payne had come into contact with the enemy while serving with Yates' Sharpshooters near New Madrid, Missouri. Writing to his grandfather, he expressed satisfaction with his reaction under fire: "I was surprised at myself when the guns began to play upon us & shots were falling all around that I did not become more flurried & excited, though I thought I stood a good chance to make Mo. my resting place for the first two or three shots—after that I hardly thought of dainger & was perfectly cool and self possessed."[16] A few weeks later, however, as his unit advanced into Mississippi, Payne took the precaution of making out "my final & only Will & Testament." Leading the 124th OVI into the Battle of Chickamauga

Opposite: Sheet music and other memorabilia commemorate the volunteers known as "Squirrel Hunters," who came from all corners of Ohio to defend Cincinnati against an apprehended attack by a Confederate force in Kentucky. They marched across the Ohio River and built fortifications, but the rebels failed to show.

in September 1863, he came close to activating it. "I am badly but not danger-ously wounded," he tersely wired to his father two days later from Chattanooga.[17] "The early loss of the Col., at a moment of great danger was most keenly felt by the Regt. and can not be too sincerely deplored," wrote the regiment's acting commander in his report. "Unbounded confidence was felt in his skill and cour-age, and his gallant conduct during the brief exposure before his wound, gave evidence of what might have been expected in the subsequent encounters."[18]

Serving with the 7th OVI at Antietam, Morris Holly also earned his "red badge of courage" in one of the bloodiest battles of the war. In a letter addressed to the editor of the *Leader,* he described his regiment's role. The 7th found itself in thick underbrush facing the enemy on "a smal eminence on which was a stone Wall behind which they took shelter," when the order came to charge. "I have seen Charges made before by old Soldiers but nothing could surpass The *Ohio boys* in This Charge—each man sprung to his feet and with a wild yell rushed forward upon the foe," wrote Holly. "Bayonets clashed for a moment or two, when the rebels took to their heels in great disorder leaving behind piles of dead and wounded and some two hundred prisoners[.] I saw no more[,] I received a ball near my knee joint during the Bayonett charge which has prevented me from sharing with my Regt. the desperate fight on Wednesday in which They suffered severly [*sic*]."[19] Costly as it was, Antietam was enough of a Northern victory to persuade President Lincoln that the time had come to issue a Preliminary Eman-cipation Proclamation.

For the most part, Ohioans on the home front had to content themselves with such vicarious accounts of the war written by participants from far-flung battlefields. On only three occasions did the conflict actually threaten or impinge on Ohio territory. In 1862 came the "Siege of Cincinnati," when Confederate general Kirby Smith defeated a Union force in Kentucky and advanced with his small army on Ohio's defenseless Queen City. Responding to Gov. David Tod's call for volunteers, more than 15,000 farmers, mechanics, clerks, and laborers descended on Cincinnati with whatever weapons were at hand. Nearly 3,000 of these "Squirrel Hunters," as they were immortalized by one contemporary observer, came all the way from the Western Reserve. Placed under the command of Maj. Gen. Lew Wallace, they crossed the Ohio River into Kentucky and began throwing up earthworks against the invader. Kirby's force never came within sight of these improvised defenses, and the soil of Ohio remained inviolate.

The following year, however, a force of 2,400 mounted Confederates conduct-ed a raid into Ohio under the command of Col. John Hunt Morgan. Crossing the Ohio River into Indiana, Morgan's force turned east and entered Ohio on July 13, 1863. As the raiders passed through the northern suburbs of Cincinnati, Governor Tod called out the Squirrel Hunters once again, while Union regulars followed in pursuit. Morgan's men continued across southern Ohio, stealing horses, pillag-

ing towns, and tearing up railroad tracks. By the time they were ready to recross the Ohio River at Buffington Island, however, Union forces and gunboats had converged to block their way. Some surrendered while Morgan led the remnant northward in search of a crossing. He did not find one, as he and his last 400 men were forced to surrender in Columbiana County. Only twenty-five miles or so south of the Western Reserve, this marked the northernmost point of Confederate penetration during the Civil War. Sent to the Ohio Penitentiary in Columbus, Morgan escaped only to die a year later in a skirmish in Tennessee.

Finally, Ohio was the target of a plot in 1864 to establish a Confederate Department of the Northwest with freed Southern prisoners of war. It was the brainchild of Capt. Charles H. Cole, an officer under Gen. Nathan B. Forrest, who planned to capture a Union Great Lakes gunboat, the USS *Michigan,* and use it to force the release of 2,700 Confederate officers being held on Johnson's Island in Sandusky Bay. The freed rebels would then commandeer a train to take them to Columbus, where they would release another 5,000 prisoners from Camp Chase and then return to capture Sandusky and use it as their base of military operations. Cole was on the verge of executing the first phase of his plan, the capture of the *Michigan,* when it was betrayed by one of the prisoners on Johnson's Island. Although a fellow plotter was hanged, Cole eventually received a presidential pardon for his part in what entered Civil War lore as "the Lake Erie Conspiracy."

Nearly 3,000 captured Confederate officers were held by the Union in a prisoner-of-war camp on Johnson's Island in Sandusky Bay. An abortive plot by a Confederate agent to free them became known in Civil War annals as "the Lake Erie Conspiracy." The island is now connected by a recently constructed causeway to the Marblehead peninsula.

Like many young northern Ohioans, Peter M. Hitchcock postponed marriage to enlist in the Union Army where he saw active service in the Battles of Shiloh and Vicksburg. He returned to marry the girl he left behind, Sara Jane Wilcox, and engaged in manufacturing in Cleveland, where he became a founder of the Reliance Electric Company.

Such local incidents, of course, were no more than sideshows to the major battles in the South that decided the outcome of the war. Ohioan Peter M. Hitchcock was an eyewitness to one of the war's turning points. An iron worker from Youngstown, he postponed his marriage to his sweetheart, Sara Jane Wilcox, to enlist in the army early in 1861. A year later he sent his father an American flag he had retrieved from a muddy corn crib on the battlefield at Shiloh. Another year had passed when on July 4, 1863, he sent Sara news that promised to bring their marriage date closer. "My own Sara," he began, "Vicksburgh [*sic*] is ours! Pemberton surrendered this morning at 10 o'clock. . . . The surrender was unconditional, but Gen Grant informed Gen Pemberton that he should parole the men, and that the field officers should be entitled to take one horse each with them, and all officers retain their side arms."[20] That was all he had time to write, as Hitchcock had fifteen miles of hard riding ahead to get back to his brigade from Vicksburg.

Simultaneous Union victories at Vicksburg and Gettysburg decided the issue of the war, but nearly two years of desperate fighting remained before the Confederacy was compelled to surrender. During Grant's spring offensive against Lee in 1864, Ohio governor John Brough came up with a plan to release more of Grant's men for combat duty. Meeting with his counterparts from Indiana, Illinois, Iowa, and Wisconsin, Brough proposed that together they should offer President Lincoln 85,000 volunteers for 100 days' garrison duty behind the lines. Ohio's quota of these "Hundred Days' Men" would be 30,000, to be raised from discharged and wounded veterans and men above and below military age. Nathan Payne was one of them, much to his younger brother's uneasiness. Hearing that some of the Hundred Days' volunteers had asked to be sent to the front, Oliver wrote that he hoped Nathan would "in no consideration place yrself in danger—you owe it to our parents, it is enough for them to have one son exposed."[21] Ohio surpassed its quota by raising 35,892 of these temporaries. Many of them were exposed to fire, but Nathan Payne survived his experience.

While Grant hammered away at Lee in Virginia, Gen. William Tecumseh Sherman, another Ohioan, took the war into the deep South. With him was Henry C. Martindale of Kirtland, who had enlisted in the 1st Ohio Volunteer Light Artillery in 1862. Sixty years later *Plain Dealer* reporter Bruce Catton (who went on to enjoy a distinguished career as a Civil War historian) tracked him down in Cleveland to record his memories. "Ordinarily, you know, when you're in a battle you can't see a thing except what's right in front of you, and you can't give much of an account of things," he told Catton. "But I saw the whole of Lookout Mountain and Mission[ary] ridge, in Tennessee." He stayed with Sherman's Army of the Tennessee to the end. "The march to the sea was just one long picnic. . . . Our orders were to destroy everything that might give aid and comfort to the enemy, and we certainly did it." Martindale maintained that there was "mighty little" wanton destruction of property all the way through Georgia. "It was different when we got

Among the fortunate Civil War veterans to come marching home were these survivors of the 23rd Ohio Volunteer Infantry, shown here on Public Square prior to being mustered out at Camp Cleveland. They had fought at the Battle of Antietam, pursued the Confederates in Morgan's Raid, and participated in Sheridan's Shenandoah Valley campaign. Its ranks produced five future Civil War generals and two U.S. presidents.

up into South Carolina, though," admitted Martindale. "We felt that that was the birthplace of the rebellion, so we let them have it."[22]

But not all Buckeyes in blue were around to tell their tales. Alexander Varian Jr., son of the Episcopalian rector, had a close call when struck by a rifle ball at Missionary Ridge. "It passed through the pocket of my overcoat," he wrote, "going through a letter of [his sisters] Mary's and Laura's which I had received 2 days before, went through my meerschaum pipe, breaking the latter all to pieces and finally flattenned out my bell plate[,] bending it. It knocked me down knocking the breath out of me." Coming to, Varian conducted a self-examination and discovered nothing worse than a painful "black and blue spot on my stomach the size of my hand."[23] Six months later, he took a bullet in the chest during a charge in the Battle of Resaca in Georgia. Nothing broke the impact this time, and Varian died two weeks later. For him and some 35,000 Ohioans, the road to freedom proved a hard one indeed.

THE EMANCIPATION OF THE NEGROES, JANUARY, 1863—THE PAST AND THE FUTURE.—Drawn by Mr. Thomas Nast—[See Page]

Harper's Weekly celebrated the dawn of emancipation in this issue of early January 1863. Cleveland organized two jubilee meetings, one for the general population and the other organized by the city's "colored citizens."

Life on
the Home Front

THE EMANCIPATION PROCLAMATION, published in the local newspapers on Saturday, January 3, 1863, galvanized the local black community into joyful action and rekindled the debate between the Republican newspapers, the *Herald* and the *Leader,* and the Democratic *Plain Dealer,* which would continue into the fall through the bitter and acrimonious gubernatorial election. On January 12 the announcement appeared in the *Leader* that Frederick Douglass would speak on the subject, "The Proclamation," at Chapin's Hall at 7:30 P.M. on January 15. A capacity crowd paid twenty-five cents' admission to hear America's most renowned former slave. "He began by congratulating his friends and fellow-citizens that a colored skin is no longer a badge of slavery in the United States, and that the Emancipation Proclamation of President Lincoln and the opinion of U.S. Attorney Bates declar [*sic*] that the colored man may claim to be an American citizen," summarized the *Leader.*[1]

Douglass repeated his remarks the following night at a jubilee organized by Cleveland's "colored citizens" in National Hall. "The night was stormy, and pedestrianism difficult on account of the deep snow, yet the hall was packed," noted the *Leader.* Behind the speakers were "two full length portraits of an African," one depicting him in chains and the other with broken shackles at his side and hands uplifted in thanks toward heaven. Looming above the stage was a portrait of John Brown. Before speaking, Douglass asked the assembly to rise in singing "The Year of Jubilee Has Come." Among the other speakers were two black men from Oberlin. Former rescuer John Watson recited a firsthand account of the Oberlin-Wellington Rescue that had so stirred northern Ohio four years earlier. He was followed by J. M. Langston, who "consumed much of his time in advocating the right and duty of colored men, to stand on the battle field alongside of their pale-faced brethren, and fight against the enemies of their country, for it is their country now."[2]

Former slave Frederick Douglass was the principal speaker at both of Cleveland's gatherings in celebration of Lincoln's Emancipation Proclamation. Traveling through Ohio some fifteen years earlier, he had described the state as "disgraced by her villainous black laws."

The celebrations over, the black community got to work to petition governor David Tod to establish an Ohio regiment for Negro soldiers. Tod still was reluctant, but Massachusetts had gained permission to organize the 54th Massachusetts Colored Troops and was recruiting all through the North. John Malvin in Cleveland, Charles Langston in Oberlin, and John M. Langston in Cincinnati all recruited for the 54th in Ohio, participating in a network of recruiters that included Frederick Douglass. It was not until late spring that Governor Tod was persuaded that not only was he losing black Ohioans to Massachusetts and other states, but those states were gaining credits toward their draft quotas while Ohio was losing them. Consequently Tod authorized the establishment of the 124th Regiment of Ohio Volunteers, which was to be a colored regiment and was eventually mustered in as the 5th U.S. Colored Troops. A special camp was set up just southeast of Columbus, Camp Delaware, where the newly organized regiment began its training.

Throughout the summer and fall of 1863, while black troops were pouring into and training at Camp Delaware, a constant stream of stories appeared in newspapers across the state telling how well disciplined and well drilled these black soldiers were and, when on leave, how polite. It was as if they had read and absorbed the earlier self-help words of *The Aliened American* on "how to act like a gentleman." This was a carefully orchestrated campaign to combat the charges and the fears inflamed by the Democratic press and the Copperhead gubernatorial campaign of Clement L. Vallandigham, which charged that Negroes were inherently undisciplined and would make terrible soldiers and disgrace the flag. Once armed, it was further alleged, they would become predatory marauders against white communities. The race card was blatantly played in the mid-nineteenth century.

There could be few worse offenders than the *Cleveland Plain Dealer* in whipping up racial hatred and fear. During the election of 1860, editor Joseph Gray had never missed a chance to portray the Republicans as the party whose victory would lead to the end of slavery and the beginning of racial equality. He continued singing the same tune through the first year of the war. A pair of miscegenation incidents, one in Cleveland and the other in Detroit, brought a warning from the editor in the fall of 1861. "We do believe," said the *Plain Dealer,* "that if the African Gorilla was plenty in our midst, 'lying around loose' like many of these worthless negroes, they would have no trouble in contracting 'advantageous family alliances,' among some of our women!"[3]

Yet Gray, unlike his successor John S. Stephenson, was a shrewd newspaperman who had kept the *Plain Dealer* solvent as a Democratic organ in a Whig, and then Republican-dominated, region. Even after the death of his political icon Stephen A. Douglas in 1861, Gray continued to uphold Douglas's policy in the *Plain Dealer* of supporting the Union while opposing the Republicans. Not the least of his talents was in recruiting bright, young talent, the most famous of whom was Charles Farrar Browne. A gawky, unkempt stripling from Waterford, Maine, Browne came to Ohio with his parents and worked for newspapers in Tiffin and Toledo before he was hired by Gray on October 30, 1857. He wrote contemporary political and social satire through the guise of "Artemus Ward," itinerant showman and waxworks proprietor. His letters, stories, and lectures in purposely labored English were precursors of the kind of down-home, Yankee humor that

Joseph W. Gray founded the *Cleveland Plain Dealer* in 1842 and kept the Democratic daily alive for two decades as "a voice in the wilderness of Whiggery" and, later, republicanism. Through virulently against abolitionism, he faithfully supported the Union war effort until his death in 1862.

Racial prejudices at first led Ohio to reject the enlistment of blacks in the state's regiments. Only after other states began accepting black Ohioans in their units, and thereby lowering their own draft quotas, did Ohio relent and begin organizing its own colored regiments. As indicated in this recruiting poster from Pennsylvania, most black regiments were trained and led by white officers.

COME AND JOIN US BROTHERS.

PUBLISHED BY THE SUPERVISORY COMMITTEE FOR RECRUITING COLORED REGIMENTS
1210 CHESTNUT ST. PHILADELPHIA.

Mark Twain later perfected—and also the kind of humor that Abraham Lincoln practiced and enjoyed. When Browne got around to publishing his work in *Artemus Ward: His Book* in the spring of 1862, Lincoln read some of the stories aloud to his cabinet. Lincoln, in fact, perhaps to the consternation of his more stuffy cabinet members such as Secretary of the Treasury Salmon P. Chase, insisted on reading a story by Artemus Ward prior to reading his Preliminary Emancipation Proclamation for their reactions.

Perhaps the one on "Oberlin" was a little too sensitive for the solemn occasion at hand. ("But its my onbiassed 'pinion that they go it rather too strong on Ethiopians at Oberlin," says Ward. "But that's nun of my bizness. I'm into the show bizness."[4]) Instead, most witnesses agree that Lincoln turned to the sketch entitled "High-Handed Outrage at Utica":

In the faul of 1856, I showed my show in Utiky, a trooly grate sitty in the State of New York.

The people gave me a cordyal recepshun. The press was loud in her prases.

1 day as I was givin a descripshun of my Beests and Snaiks in my usual flowry stile what was my skorn & disgust to see a big burly feller walk up to the cage containin my wax figgers of the Lord's Last Supper, and cease Judas Iscarrot by the feet and drag him out on the ground. He then commenced fur to pound him as hard as he cood.

"What under the son are you abowt?" cried I.

Sez he, "What did you bring this pussylanermus cuss here fur?" & he hit the wax figger another tremenjis blow on the hed.

Sez I, "You egrejus ass, that air's a wax figger—a representashun of the false 'Postle."

Sez he, "That's all very well fur you to say but I tell you, old man, that Judas Iscarrot can't show hisself in Utiky with impunerty by a darn site!" with which observashun he kaved in Judassis hed. The young man belonged to 1 of the first famerlies in Utiky. I sood him, and the Joory brawt in a verdick of Arson in the 3d degree.[5]

One of the most brilliant journalists ever to practice in Cleveland was Charles Farrar Browne, a droll stripling from Maine. Though his stint as local editor of the *Plain Dealer* lasted only three years, it was memorable for Browne's creation of a fictitious alter ego named Artemus Ward. He left Cleveland in 1860, spending most of his remaining seven years on the lecture circuit.

Ushered in by the issuance of Lincoln's Emancipation Proclamation, 1863 would prove as momentous a year for the whole city of Cleveland as it was for its black community. By 1863 most northern Ohioans settled into a daily routine, accepting with equanimity and some guilt such privations and demands that the war brought. As mayor Irvine U. Masters reflected in his annual message to the City Council on April 18, 1864, "Our community has not directly felt the shock of war. On the contrary, all departments of business have been in active and successful operation. The material elements of prosperity have largely increased. The population of our city has steadily and rapidly increased to such a degree that its present accomodations are entirely insufficient. Individual families have indeed been reminded by the sad bereavements, or longing absence of loved ones, that war, in all its cruel and desolating power is raging in the land."[6] These sentiments were privately expressed by Elizabeth Bingham to her husband William, partner in the George Worthington Company, Cleveland's largest hardware and commission house, who was in New York City on a buying trip. "My dear William," she wrote not long after the excitement of Morgan's Raid, "I'm glad we're to have something that looks a little war-like. Can it be we are to live through this rebellion, and see nothing of it! living as peacefully in our own times as ever. It *does* seem as though we were more blessed than others."[7]

Women carried most of the burden of the war on the home front, while men who were not in service carried on business and politics as usual. Dr. Myra K. Merrick had established a thriving medical practice among the most influential women in the community, but when her husband, Charles, enlisted in the 8th Ohio Volunteer Infantry Regiment early in 1861, she took over the running of the family lumber business and did so throughout the war. Merrick was an unusual woman. She was born in England and grew up in Massachusetts, where she worked in cotton mills. Moving with her parents to Elyria in the early 1840s, Myra met and married Charles H. Merrick and then moved back to Connecticut. There she began studying medicine, sitting in on lectures and finally taking an M.D. degree at Central Medical College in Rochester, New York. The Merricks

Nancie Swan, a Medina County schoolteacher, expressed conflicted emotions in her weekly diary entries. Though she wished she might have enlisted herself, she became distraught at hearing of the enlistment of her brother Charles. She also balanced a desire for personal independence against a growing apprehension that she was fated to remain a spinster.

moved back to Cleveland in the 1850s. Alone during the war, she carried on her practice, the lumber business, and raised her two sons, all the while reading the outpourings of her soldier-husband and carefully saving his letters. She also organized a Ladies' Aid Society to furnish volunteer nurses to the U.S. Army General Hospital at Camp Cleveland.

Viewing the war from a more commonplace vantage point was Nancie Swan, an unmarried teacher in various Medina County schools. In 1860 she lived with her widowed father, an unsuccessful farmer, and younger brother, Charlie. A faithful, if not eloquent, Sunday-night diarist, she was not immediately touched by war; in fact, in the spring of 1861 she was preparing for an extended visit with her older brother, Jim, and sister-in-law in Minnesota. She did note in April, however, "Today the volunteers left town for Cleveland. It was a sad sight to see them start away[,] though perhaps not to meet real danger yet to encounter hardships and uncertainties at least."[8] A few days later she was on her way with a group of young women to visit the recruits at Camp Taylor. "We arrived at the Bennett House at four o'clock where we all put up. We went out to the Camp as soon as we could hail a car. We found but few of our company's men though we stayed till six o'clock."[9]

Nancie's year in Minnesota proved to be one of boredom and tedium. Her diary is filled with entries about paring bees for drying apples for the troops, berrying parties in the summer, but none of these activities seemed to catch her fancy. She had read of the disaster at Bull Run, noting that "The victory was with the rebels and many of our brave soldiers fell. It has cast a gloom over everyone but still we are far from despairing. Oh! How I felt for the friends of those engaged! It is rather strange that in all this I only think of Charlie [her younger brother] and realize how I should feel if he was with them."[10] Then the war did touch her, as she received news that Charlie had enlisted. "I have said so much against his enlisting," she wrote in September. "It seems selfish that we are making no sacrifice, not that I would sacrifice any of my friends but if I could only go myself and be of any use, I believe I would even to the laying down of life. But here I must remain quietly inactive without ever seeing much done for the support of war."[11]

The following year Nancie was either teaching or seeking a teaching position in one of the many small schools in the townships dotting Medina County. After attending the funeral of a local soldier in November she wondered, "How many more[,] oh: how many must fall beneath this sad and miserable scourge of our land. Today Mr. Varney's son who fell at the battle of Antietam was again reburied here. This is the third son who has fallen in the same family."[12] Charlie, however, was mustered out of service after his hundred-day enlistment was up. "He shall not go to war again if it is possible for me to help it," wrote Nancie. "I will work in some one's kitchen to procure money to buy him off. Oh if I could only go in his place[,] how willingly I would do it! How soon—were I a man I should know what to do with myself now."[13]

For Nancie Swan 1863 was a year filled with momentous events, not all connected to the war. On March 29, 1863, she recorded, "Today is my twenty-fifth birthday and I am now an 'old maid'! Nancie B. Swan[,] spinster. . . . A quarter of a century[,] more than a third of the alloted life of mortals and still I am careless[,] heedless that the time is speeding one along to my sure destiny be it sooner or later." The cultural and familial pressures for young women to marry and to do so at a young age were tremendous, and not all were comfortable with the idea. Nancie would later muse, "I wish marriage was not the ultimatum of all young ladies for indeed it is a real bore to think that I must come to that or be a nonentity in [the] social world."[14] Of course the war was partially responsible for her situation, since the pool of young marriageable men had been seriously diminished as they left for the front, sometimes singing the popular tune, "The Girl I Left Behind Me." Nancie moved to Montville, her hometown, to take a teaching job at nearby Coddingville and lived in a rented room in a friend's house. This she did with no great enthusiasm. "I dread the idea of teaching & boarding around even among friends . . . but it is no worse for me than others & I have no right to any better home."[15]

In September, however, such thoughts were pushed aside when Capt. Porter Foskett came to town on furlough after the Vicksburg campaign to renew his acquaintance with Nancie. The two had known each other before the war; Nancie had been a teacher at the Coddingville school when it closed with the outbreak of

Before reading his Preliminary Emancipation Proclamation to his cabinet, president Abraham Lincoln lightened the mood by reading them a selection from the recently published *Artemus Ward: His Book* by former Clevelander Charles F. Browne. Many of the sketches in the book had originally appeared in Browne's *Plain Dealer* column. Seated (left to right) are Edwin M. Stanton, Lincoln, Gideon Welles, William Seward, and Edward Bates; standing are Salmon P. Chase, Caleb Smith, and Montgomery Blair.

While her husband and son served in the Union Army, Marilla Wells Leggett remained in Zanesville to care for her other children and help organize Soldiers' Aid Society activities on the home front. Twice she traveled to visit her husband, Mortimer, in the field in Mississippi. Her experiences, both in the South and back home, were faithfully recorded in her diaries.

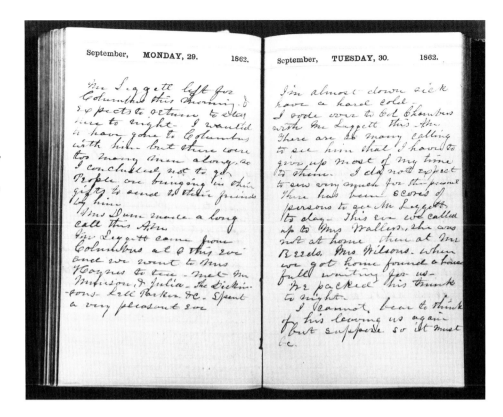

war and Porter enlisted in the 42nd Ohio Volunteer Infantry Regiment forming at Camp Chase in Columbus. At the time Porter had been simply one of a number of Nancie's male acquaintances, but with wartime pressures and heightened emotions, not to mention Nancie's acute awareness of her growing spinsterhood, it is not strange that the relationship became more serious.

One day they took a carriage trip to Lima to visit her brother Charlie. Still concerned about her independent status, Nancie tried to insist on bearing her share of the expenses but was quickly silenced by Porter. "Coming home I was so sleepy that when he drew my head down on his shoulder to rest me I did not resist and at last I let him press kiss after kiss upon lips and cheek without any of that feeling of repugnance which I had felt the day before at his lightest touch or look," she confided on a note of perplexity. "Why is this and what will he think of me for such conduct when he calls me to account for it as perhaps he may before leaving."[16] Nevertheless, as soon as he left she was looking for letters from him.

Marilla Wells Leggett's diary during these years reflects the wartime experience of a different group of northern Ohioans. Like most women of her time, Marilla had no profession other than wife and mother. She had grown up in northern Ohio near Kirtland and married Mortimer Leggett at the age of twenty. Mortimer, a graduate of Kirtland Teachers' Seminary, was admitted to the bar in 1844 and graduated from Willoughby Medical College in 1845. He practiced law for a time in Warren with Jacob Cox, who may have helped him later to obtain a commission in the army. In the 1850s he was an innovative school superintendent in Warren and in Akron, where he was instrumental in developing the free, graded, public school system. He moved on to take the superintendency of schools in Zanesville, which is where Marilla found herself at the outbreak of war.

As superintendent of schools, Mortimer Leggett was an instant community leader; and Marilla, in spite of family duties (she had four young children), was also an active participant in community affairs: church work, sewing circles, and even politics. Late in 1861, after Lincoln's call for 300,000 three-year volunteers, Leggett took it upon himself to raise a regiment in Zanesville. A temporary camp was hastily constructed on the outskirts of town in October. The Leggett house became a sort of headquarters away from camp, and all during the war Marilla's house was open to women of the community seeking information and comfort.

By early January 1862, the 78th OVI had a full complement of men and was ready to move to Camp Chase in Columbus to be mustered into the United States Army. Mortimer Leggett, elected lieutenant colonel of the regiment, had received orders to be ready to march at six hours' notice. Orders to move finally came on February 10: "About one o'clock Mortimer came in and said they had orders to be off just as soon as possible. This gave us quite a shock, but we went to work some at one thing, and some at another." The rest of the day was spent drying and ironing clothes to be taken to camp and making ginger cakes at Mortimer's request. That night, Mortimer's last at home, he and Marilla "talked most all night. At two we wakened & talked matters over, arranged affairs a little, & at 5 o'clock he bade us farewell. I had no idea that I should feel so badly, for I

Seated (second from left) with his staff is Maj. Gen. Mortimer D. Leggett, who entered the Civil War as colonel of the 78th Ohio Volunteer Infantry. After the war Leggett was one of the founders of the Brush Electric Company in Cleveland.

A major undertaking of the Soldiers' Aid Society of Northern Ohio was the construction of a Soldiers' Home near Cleveland's Union Depot. The narrow wooden building was divided into a dining hall and a ward where Union troops might be lodged and fed as they passed through the city on their way home or back to the front. Wounded soldiers also received medical attention in the infirmary.

have been trying to nerve myself up for the trying hour but I could not control my feelings at all. They controlled me."[17] Mortimer and his oldest son, Wells, left with the rest of the regiment the following day.

The 78th OVI moved immediately into Kentucky to join Grant's siege of Fort Donelson on the Cumberland River at the very center of the Confederate line holding Kentucky and western Tennessee. Marilla received a dispatch from Leggett on February 15, informing her that they were about to start up the Cumberland. "We are exceedingly pleased to hear from them," she commented. "They seem to be going in the direction of something to do[.]"[18] Two days later she heard of the taking of Fort Donelson with 15,000 Confederate prisoners. "I'm very anxious to hear whether our men were there," she worried. "I want to hear from them more than ever."[19] Later she learned that the surrender had taken place only hours before the 78th had reached the battlefield.

Through 1862 Marilla had acted as the fount of news about the 78th and the men of the families of Zanesville. She sewed for the Soldiers' Aid Society and baked for its benefit picnics. In July Mortimer wrote that he could not get home but asked Marilla to come visit him, and she "concluded to do so." "Hurrah for starting for Dixie Land this eve.," she recorded on July 14. "Almost everybody we know have called in to see us today." She rode in a boxcar with several other women going to see friends or loved ones in the army, there being no passenger cars available. Marilla returned after nearly a month in the heart of Mississippi with her husband, while the 78th moved on toward Vicksburg. Awaiting her back in Zanesville were such motherly functions as tearfully accompanying her youngest son Marcellus off to school for the first time, canning fruits in the fall for the

Soldiers' Aid Society, and ensuring that Santa Claus gave the children a joyous Christmas. "The old year closes tonight," she observed on December 31, "and the year has been a very sad one to most of us—A great many hearts have been made sad by disasters that have befallen our Country, and the prospect is very dark for the future."

Marilla's dark forebodings about the war might well have included her family's future as well as her country's. As with Nancie Swan, 1863 would see personal events compounding the abiding sorrows and privations of war. Marilla was five months' pregnant (the child was conceived during her month-long trip to visit Mortimer in Mississippi in the summer of 1862), and the baby was due some time in April. Brig. Gen. Mortimer Leggett asked for and received leave from his duties at the siege of Vicksburg to go home to be with his wife during her confinement. An entry signed "M.D.L." appears in the diary dated Tuesday, April 28, 1863: "Mrs. Leggett was confined to day and gave birth to a noble great 12 pound boy a few minutes before midnight." He left to join his brigade a few weeks later.

Marilla was confined to her bed for nearly a month, lonely, nervous, and depressed. Her spirits were somewhat lifted on May 25 by news of Grant's capture of Vicksburg, but the report proved to be considerably premature. Instead, she read a few days later in the *Cincinnati Gazette* that Mortimer was among a group of officers wounded in the siege of Vicksburg. "I can scarcely content myself to wait till Monday to hear the particulars," she fretted.[20] Eventually she learned that her husband had received two wounds, neither of them life threatening, "and had lost from that brigade over 400 men—and some of whom we are acquainted."[21]

Through it all Marilla had a household to run, a task made more difficult by scarcity of food and resources and rising prices. And early in June the baby boy got sick and became progressively worse. Marilla got little sleep for the next ten days. On Monday, July 13, 1863, she made the somber entry: "He died at 15

With tables constantly set in readiness for incoming trains, the dining hall in the Soldiers' Home provided more than 100,000 meals for Northern troops passing through Cleveland. Service was almost nonstop for homeward-bound veterans at the close of the war.

minutes past 5 P.M." The community of friends and neighbors flooded the house with words of condolence and support. Marilla recovered quickly and planned a trip in the fall to Vicksburg to visit Mortimer, whose wound turned out to be more serious than he had let on. His right arm was paralyzed, but Marilla at least had the comfort of spending the closing months of the year with her husband and son Wells.

Rebecca Rouse, a vigorous sixty-two, no longer had childcare worries, but her life was consumed by the ever-growing responsibilities of the massive Soldiers' Aid Society of Northern Ohio, the Cleveland branch of the United States Sanitary Commission. Mrs. Rouse was certainly up to the task. Although "short and slight . . . her strength seemed to be in inverse ratio to her size. She never seemed tired, though she worked continually."[22] After the news of the defeat at Bull Run, she realized that the activities of the Soldiers' Aid Society would have to be stepped up and expanded. The unfocused activities of the volunteer ladies, in order to be effective, would have to be centralized and to some degree standardized. She sent out a circular to the postmasters and ministers all over the state asking for support and for the names of six actively benevolent women who might be willing to organize a local aid society.

Soon the Cleveland society had an active correspondence with women all around northern Ohio who had turned their sewing circles and literary groups into local aid societies. Cleveland, of course, was a natural hub for the reception of supplies, sorting, and redistribution, with rail connections radiating out and connecting the other communities throughout northern Ohio. Realizing that this was to be a regional effort, the members of the Soldiers' Aid Society quickly changed its name to the Soldiers' Aid Society of Northern Ohio, and in the fall

Depicted on the fair's letterhead was the temporary wooden hall erected in the winter of 1864 for the Northern Ohio Sanitary Fair. Though the background appears rustic, the cruciform structure was actually located in the middle of Public Square. In just eighteen days the event raised $78,000 for the activities of the Soldiers' Aid Society of Northern Ohio.

of 1862 affiliated with the United States Sanitary Commission. Although private, the Sanitary Commission had the sanction of the Federal government. Its agents inspected the conditions and needs of army hospitals in the war zones, acting as official liaisons between the army and local volunteer societies.

Mrs. Rouse met with women in the surrounding communities to help them organize or simply urge them to greater effort. When she was not working with her staff of volunteers at the rented store at 95 Bank Street, next to the American Express Company, she was traveling, making speeches, giving instruction, and helping to organize. By the end of 1863, 150 local aid societies as far east as Meadville, Pennsylvania, and as far west as Sandusky were affiliated with the Cleveland group.

Caroline Younglove, daughter of papermill owner M. C. Younglove and self-described "general utility girl . . . ready for anything she could turn her hand to, from rolling bandages and picking lint, to bathing the brow of the first good looking soldier who should present himself,"[23] later described the activities that went on for four years at 95 Bank Street. Caroline thought it was "to our Secretary, Miss Brayton (Dear Miss Maggie, as I always think of her) that most of our success was due. She had remarkable executive ability, and it was her clear head and good judgment which carried us triumphantly through every emergency as it arose."[24] Indeed, Mary Clark Brayton later wrote a lively, detailed account of the society's activities, *Our Acre and Its Harvest.* In the book she detailed the stores that trickled into the Bank Street office from outlying farms and villages, from socks, shirts, and hand-decorated pillows to jars of fruit preserves. Some items of apparel came with personal notes attached for the anonymous recipients, such as

Brave sentry, on your lonely beat,
    May these blue stockings warm your feet,
And when from wars and camps you part,
    May some fair knitter warm your heart.[25]

When reports came from the field of outbreaks of scurvy among the troops, the society emulated the "blanket raid" of the war's early days with a "vegetable raid." This time the women didn't have to go out and scour the countryside; all they had to do was get out word of the need. "A crossroads settlement sent as one installment twenty-eight barrels of potatoes," recorded Mary Clark Brayton. "Every town within shipping distance of Cleveland sent again and again its offering."[26] And not content to remain on the home front, Miss Brayton also managed to visit the troops in the field. "Yesterday I was very agreeably surprised by a visit from Miss Maggie Brayton," Oliver Payne reported from Franklin, Tennessee, in 1863. "Miss Brayton took us by surprise and found us just as we always live." After having dinner with Payne and bringing him up to date on hometown news, she

The keynote speaker at the opening of the Northern Ohio Sanitary Fair was former major general and newly elected U.S. congressman James A. Garfield. "There is something behind bayonets," he declared, in paying tribute to the efforts of women on the home front in support of the troops in the field.

left him wondering why "more of the Cleveland ladies do not occasionally visit the army."[27]

In 1863 the biggest project of the ladies of the Soldiers' Aid Society of Northern Ohio was to build and maintain a Soldiers' Home. The Cleveland, Columbus & Cincinnati Railroad donated a site a few yards west of its Lakeside Depot. The need was sufficiently urgent and specific that the ladies decided on a personal solicitation of businessmen rather than the traditional and more genteel circular and mail appeals. Free utilities were pledged by the gas and water companies, and a local doctor provided beds. By early December a long, wooden, barracks-like building, 22 feet wide by 200 feet long and later to be extended, was up and ready for business. It was divided into a dining hall with two rows of tables set perpendicular to the outside wall with a central serving aisle. The tables were set with tablecloths, knives, forks and spoons, and china plates. In the ward section, twenty-five "well fitted out" beds were ready to receive wounded travelers.

The idea was to be able to dress and rebandage the wounds of soldiers en route home or to the hospital. Meals and temporary lodging were also provided for soldiers on furlough or returning home after honorable discharge. "At the close of the war," recalled Caroline Younglove Abbott, "we fed here train after train of returning regiments. . . . A train load of seven or eight hundred men would no sooner be cared for and sent on their way with ringing cheers, when another would be signalled and we would have to reset the tables. . . . To those who were too ill to leave the train the ladies would go and carry help and comfort."[28] By the end of the war Mary Clark Brayton proudly recorded that "fifty-seven thousand six hundred and nine soldiers found temporary shelter there, to whom one hundred and eleven thousand nine hundred and one meals, and seventy-nine thousand nine hundred and seventy-four lodgings were given."[29]

An undertaking on the scale of the Soldiers' Home entailed financial obligations unimagined back in the improvised "blanket raid" phase of the Soldiers' Aid Society. Seeking means of supporting the home and their other activities, officers of the northern Ohio group went to investigate a fair organized by their Chicago counterparts in September 1863. With the aid of Lincoln's donation for auction of his personal copy of the Emancipation Proclamation, the Chicagoans raised $100,000 for the cause. The Clevelanders came home with even more ambitious plans for their own exhibition.

In a circular issued from 95 Bank Street on November 24, Rebecca Rouse and her officers announced their plans for "a Grand Festival . . . for the benefit of our sick and wounded soldiers." Due to the undiminished needs of the army and the inroads of wartime inflation, "the present year . . . finds us limited by means totally insufficient to meet the demand made upon us," stated the appeal. "The plan pursued will be similar to that of the Chicago Fair, and will comprise the sale of every variety of fancy and useful articles." Friends of the society as well as branch members were urged to contribute attractions and items for sale. Not ignoring

the social aspects of the project, the organizers noted that "aside from the pecuni-
ary benefit which we promise ourselves in this undertaking, an opportunity will
be offered to extend a cordial personal greeting to many with whom we are connected in a common cause."[30]

By the end of January, a large frame building in the form of a Greek cross was
rapidly taking shape in the center of Public Square to house the Northern Ohio
Sanitary Fair. Tickets to the affair were sold for twenty-five cents. In addition to
waiving freight charges for goods consigned to the fair, the railroads did their part
by promising half-price passenger fare for any visitors who purchased a dollar's
worth of admission tickets.

On Washington's birthday, February 22, 1864, all was ready. Rain clouds
had dispersed by nine o'clock, yielding to a bright, balmy day—"a happy omen
and augury, let us hope," said the *Leader*, "of the glad dawning of the sun of
Peace, after the clouds and storm of War." The morning train from Columbus
brought lieutenant governor Charles Anderson and members of the state legislature, who were escorted by city officials to the Weddell House for dinner. At
2 P.M. a parade headed by the 29th Ohio Volunteer Militia, "the pride of the
city," and Jack Leland's band, "breathing forth melodious and patriotic strains,"
proceeded down Superior Street to the auditorium of the Sanitary Fair for the
opening ceremonies. A ninety-minute keynote address was delivered by Maj.
Gen. James A. Garfield, hometown hero of the Battle of Chickamauga, who
had just resigned his military commission after being elected to the U.S. House

The focal point of the entire
Sanitary Fair was Floral
Hall, placed in the center of
the cruciform building and
decorated by local Cleveland
gardeners. Rather than move
the recently dedicated Perry
Monument, they raised
the domed roof sixty-five
feet over the commodore's
head and surrounded his
base with greenery. "I doubt
much if it has ever been
equaled by any thing of the
kind," said Col. Oliver H.
Payne following his visit.

One of scores of special attractions scheduled during the Northern Ohio Sanitary Fair was the Old Folk's Concert given on March 1, 1864. As suggested by this invitation, participation in the fair was a broadly based community affair. Other events included dances, drawings, and produce sales.

Cleveland, February 4, 1864.

Miss Nelly Wick

     You are respectfully invited to take part in the OLD FOLK'S CONCERT of the Northern Ohio Sanitary Fair, to be held in Cleveland, commencing February 22d, 1864.

The Concert will be given on TUESDAY, MARCH 1st, at Seven O'clock P. M.

    Rehearsals will be held at the new Court House, in Court Room, No. 3, on Tuesday Evenings, February 16th and 23d, and on Monday Evening, February 29th, all at 7 o'clock, P. M. It is desirable that all who can, should attend all the Rehearsals, but it is deemed especially important that every person should be present at the final Rehearsal on Feb. 29th, who expect to take any part at the Concert on the succeeding evening.

    Each performer is requested to appear at the Concert in Ancient Costume of their own selection. Any one desiring information with regard to costume, may consult any of the undersigned, or Mrs. SANFORD LEWIS.

    Each performer is also requested to bring with them, *if possible*, a copy of *Ancient Harmony Revived.*

    Immediately after receiving this note, you are earnestly requested to communicate to S. FOLJAMBE, Secretary of the Committee, your acceptance or otherwise of this invitation.

                  B. F. ROBINSON,
                  S. FOLJAMBE,
                  J. G. GRAHAM,
                     Committee on Old Folks Concert.

of Representatives from northern Ohio. "There is something behind bayonets," proclaimed Garfield in paying tribute to "the affections of home—the prayers and blessings of the family circle—the active assistance of the women and children left at home."[31]

That evening the halls of the fair were finally thrown open to the public. The 2,000-seat Audience Hall occupied the eastern head of the cross. In the northern arm was a 500-seat dining hall, where refreshments were available at dinner, tea, and supper hours. "Everybody dines here," wrote Mary Clark Brayton, "for Cleveland housekeepers would deem it treason to the good cause to spread any rival attractions at home."[32] The chief fundraiser of the fair was the Ladies Bazaar, located to the west at the foot of the cross, which featured booths from all the counties of northern Ohio, from Ashtabula to Ashland, along with nationality displays such as the German, with its bust of Schiller, and the Irish, with its "Erin go Bragh" in evergreen letters. Mechanics Hall occupied the southern arm and was filled with cooking stoves, wagons, sewing machines, cabinets, coal oil lamps, cider presses, steel bars, and other products of the region. A small steam engine supplied motive power for demonstrations on nail-making and knitting machines. "Each article is ticketed with the business card of the doner, and exhibiters are here to press the merits of their inventions," wrote Mary Brayton.[33] In the very center of the cross was an octagonal conservatory known as Floral Hall, which was covered by a rotunda rising sixty-five feet above the Commodore Perry Monument dedicated in Public Square three years earlier. Rather than move the monument, the planners made it the focal point of the fair, surrounding it with floral displays designed by Cleveland's leading professional gardeners. On the eastern side, for example, Theodore Shuren of Superior Street had constructed a Swiss mountainside depicting peasant cottages, flocks of goats, millstream and mill, and a basin with real fish at the bottom. "It is a better geographical study than a month over books, so far as getting an idea of the countryside is concerned," commented the *Leader*.[34]

There was more to be seen than could be accommodated in the main fair building, so the third floor of the Cuyahoga County Courthouse across the square was commandeered by the Soldiers' Aid Society for a Museum and Fine Art Hall, where both originals and copies of old masters were on view, some just for exhibit and others for sale. The originals included a portrait of Mary Queen of Scots by Holbein and one of Washington by Rembrandt Peale. Among the natural curiosities to be found in the museum was a copper axe from an Indian mound, donated by Dr. Jared Kirtland of Rockport (Lakewood). There were also rare coins, stocks and fetters from a Charleston slave pen, and "the original ordinance of secession of Louisiana." Civil War relics were in plentiful supply, too, ranging from battlefield souvenirs to the sword of a Confederate colonel hanged as a spy by Union general William Rosecrans.

For two-and-a-half weeks northern Ohioans came to the fair. A daily "Sanitary Fair Gazette" kept them informed of special attractions and events. There were dances in Floral Hall, tableaux and concerts in Audience Hall, and produce sales in Mechanics Hall. In a drawing at the Ladies Bazaar, Miss Barret of Massillon and Mrs. Captain Varner were the winners of a pair of $700 pianos.

Counting the receipts after the fair closed on March 10, the Soldiers' Aid Society came up with more than $78,000. Even the building had been sold, to be disassembled and recycled for a similar affair in Pittsburgh. But the chief contribution of the event to the war effort went beyond monetary value. Visiting the fair during his convalescence, Col. Oliver H. Payne viewed it as a satisfying demonstration of how "the whole population are sympathising with the soldiers in the field and are laboring at home in their way to facilitate the good work." Describing it for the benefit of his sister "Flo," then in Europe, Payne extolled Floral Hall as "perhaps the crowning glory of it all—nothing like it have I ever seen and I doubt much if it has ever been equalled by any thing of the kind."[35]

Indeed, the financial and spiritual uplift provided by the fair sustained the Soldiers' Aid Society of Northern Ohio to the end of the war more than a year later. They began with a capital of two dollars and closed with a cash statement of $170,000 in 1869. From a neighborhood sewing circle, it grew into a network of 525 branch organizations. It built and supported a Soldiers' Home and dispensed hospital stores valued at nearly $1 million. It sent clothing and food to soldiers in the field and gave aid and comfort to their families at home. Even after the end of hostilities, it continued as an employment service and claims agency for returning veterans. In the words of women's historian Marian J. Morton, "The challenges of the war years, met by the Sanitary Commission, prepared the next generation of women in Cleveland to organize to meet the new challenges of urban life."[36]

Most of the women of northern Ohio, of course, viewed the end of the Civil War as a return to the normal peacetime activities of home and family. It is pleasing to note that Porter Foskett returned safely to Medina County and popped the big question to the self-styled "Nancie B. Swan, spinster." In a final display of independence, she put him off for two months before finally accepting his proposal. "Frightened but calm" was the diary entry on her wedding day of October 25, 1865.

Business and Politics
—but Not as Usual

THIS MORNING I OBTAINED my first view of Atlanta," Oliver H. Payne wrote home to his father on July 6, 1864. Describing "the church spires & large buildings making a pleasant relief to the dark forest which every where seems to cover the country, with here & there a cleared crest for fortifications, with its black, savage guns relieved against the sky," Payne expressed his confident "hope to obtain a better view of Atlanta, though, at some time, not far distant."[1] Following his convalescence in Cleveland the previous winter, Payne rejoined his 124th OVI in time for Sherman's Atlanta campaign, in which the Ohio-born general skillfully maneuvered against Confederate general Joseph E. Johnston to arrive within striking distance of this gateway to the deep South. "I go back to the army with a light heart and with a mind satisfied to sacrifice my life if it is necessary," he had written earlier to his sister, Flo. "I feel most strongly that the crisis of our fate is at hand and that we stand where we must perish or succeed. Though successful in pushing the Rebels back from the sea board and the great father of Rivers, they have gathered all their strength on the rugged territory between the Cumberland mountains & the Gulf, and there must be fought the final & desperate struggle, which is to determine whether we have a country or not; in that struggle every Young man of spirit ought to be found."[2]

But having now achieved a glimpse of the end, Payne's thoughts were no longer focused exclusively on military matters. "I am glad Nathan spoke to you about obtaining some business for me & that you are giving it some thought," he told his father in that letter from the heights over Atlanta. Oliver had indeed been thinking about business for some time. More than a year earlier he had written his brother Nathan from Tennessee of the opportunities to speculate in southern cotton and tobacco, and while he would not advise Nathan to throw up the coal business in Cleveland for it, he thought his brother might dabble profitably in Tennessee tobacco as a sideline. Oliver's three years' enlistment was nearing its

Located in Newburgh, to the southeast of the city, the Cleveland Rolling Mills Co. experienced great growth during the Civil War. It was reorganized from an older firm dating from 1857 and boasted Cleveland's first blast furnace. After the war it was the first local steel concern to adopt the Bessemer process, and it eventually became absorbed into the United States Steel Corporation.

end in 1864, and he was becoming impatient to get on with his life's work. He wrote Nathan from outside Atlanta that his command had been so reduced in strength that he felt he was no longer needed. If necessary, he said, he would call on his friends in the War Department to obtain his honorable discharge, for "the life is odius to me, without a single redeeming feature to make it pleasant. . . . I have made a martyr of myself for three years—have sacrificed three of the best years of my life—is that not enough?"[3]

Payne certainly was not alone in noticing that fortunes were being made during the Civil War. "The truth is," U.S. senator John Sherman of Ohio would write to his brother, William Tecumseh, "the close of the war with our resources unimpaired gives an elevation, a scope to the ideas of leading capitalists, far higher than anything ever undertaken in this country before. They talk of millions as confidently as formerly of thousands."[4] The war itself had been responsible in large part for this great leap in fiscal imagination. Historian Allan Nevins described the primitive state of Northern industry at the beginning of the war, when one of the nation's largest hardware concerns turned out no more than 250 shovels and spades a day, and the average ironworks was capitalized at only $14,000. Following Bull Run the old scale of business was no longer suitable. A single clothing manufacturer might suddenly find itself with a contract for $1,250,000 worth of uniforms. By the final year of the conflict, the War Department was spending $431,700,000 annually, and Federal expenditures on the whole approached $1.3 billion.

Cleveland received its share in this surge of business activity, some of the first manifestations appearing in the garment industry. Not long after Fort Sumter, a local clothing establishment appealed to rampant patriotism with what has been called the first jingle in local advertising:

Yes, we'll shout at Union Hall,
Where we clothe the people all . . .
And to Buckeye boys who go,
We sell clothing very low.[5]

Prior to the war the local clothing industry had generally been run by Germans under the "family system," in which the manufacturer distributed precut parts to individual tailors to be assembled at home, often with the help of wives and children. It was the same system used by the Ladies' Aid Society early in the war to provide uniforms for the first recruits at Camp Taylor. Before long the factory system began to supplant the family system, as government-furnished measurements for standard uniform sizes led to the ready-made clothing industry. By September 1861 Davis, Peixotto and Company was filling government orders for uniforms for 500 officers and 2,000 men, and the Cleveland Worsted Mill Company was advertising for 1,000 women to knit socks for soldiers. In 1862 the German Woolen Factory began turning out the first woolen cloth manufactured in Cleveland, thus remedying a local industrial insufficiency deplored only two years earlier by Edwin Cowles in the *Leader*.

Iron and steel was another local industry jump-started during the Civil War. According to Nevins, there were only 286 furnaces in the entire country in 1860.[6] Cleveland had only three iron companies at the beginning of the war and twelve

The First National Bank of Cleveland was only the seventh in the nation created under the National Bank Act of 1863. Organized in May of that year, it was capitalized at $300,000 and occupied this dignified building at the intersection of Superior and Water (West 9th) Streets.

Daniel P. Rhodes, prospective father-in-law of young Mark Hanna, amassed his fortune in coal and railroads. He was a former business partner of David Tod of Youngstown, who was elected governor of Ohio on the Union ticket in 1861. Like Tod and Stephen A. Douglas, a distant relation, Rhodes was a Democrat in favor of maintaining the Union.

by war's end. The leading local concern was Stone, Chisholm & Jones, which built the city's first blast furnace at its Newburgh plant in 1861. Two years later the firm was reorganized by Henry Chisholm, Jeptha H. Wade, and Henry B. Payne, among others, as the Cleveland Rolling Mill Company, which would blow the area's first Bessemer process steel in 1868. By 1865 the *Cleveland Leader* reported that more than half the iron ore shipped from the Lake Superior mines was coming through Cleveland. Related industries also shared in the growth. In 1863 George Worthington and William Bingham started the Cleveland Iron & Nail Works. Coe, Ely & Harmon was formed the following year to produce hex shafts, rudder frames, and forgings for the marine trade. By 1865, 44 percent of all Great Lakes shipping was being launched from Cleveland's harbor.

According to the Cleveland Board of Trade, the value of all Cleveland manufactures rose during the Civil War from $7 million in 1860 to $39 million in 1865. Industrial expansion was facilitated by long overdue reforms in banking and finance, necessitated largely by the stresses of war. In order to finance the conflict and establish and distribute a national currency, Congress passed the National Bank Acts of 1863 and 1864. Organized on May 23, 1863, Cleveland's First National Bank was only the seventh in the country created under this act. It was capitalized at $300,000 under George Worthington as president. Two years later it was joined by the National City Bank of Cleveland, reorganized from the City Bank dating back to 1845. Capitalized at $100,000 in 1865, it listed assets of $33 billion by 1995.

The growth of local industry during the Civil War naturally opened the way to successful business careers for Cleveland's young men, especially for those who did not go to war. One of those was Mark Hanna, who paid for a substitute to serve his tour while he stayed behind to help manage the family's wholesale grocery business. As his father's health continued to deteriorate, Mark's uncle, Robert Hanna, pushed for the reorganization of Hanna, Garretson & Company Hiram Garretson's desire to branch out into the liquor trade ran counter to the temperance persuasions of the Hanna brothers. Consequently Garretson withdrew, and the *Herald* announced on December 1, 1862, the formation of R. Hanna, L. Hanna, S.H. Baird, M.A. Hanna, Robert Hanna & Company Mark Hanna was a partner and, with the death of his father Leonard only two weeks later, the sole member of his immediate family to be actively engaged in the new partnership.

If that weren't enough responsibility for the sociable young Hanna, he was soon contemplating marriage. "So Miss Rhodes is reported engaged to Hanna," Oliver Payne wrote his brother in the summer of 1864. "I fear she is not doing as well as her lovely character & beautiful face should demand. I have no high respect for Hanna."[7] Colonel Payne's low opinion of the prospective groom was undoubtedly colored by Hanna's avoidance of military service, though ironically that very summer happened to find Mark Hanna in uniform. As a member of a local militia unit known as the Perry Light Infantry, Hanna was called up as one of the "Hundred Days' Men" to provide support for Grant's army during the Wilderness campaign. Mustered into Federal service, Hanna's unit was assigned to garrison duty in the fortifications around Washington, D.C. They were there during Confederate general Jubal A. Early's assault on the city's outskirts but never came under fire.

Returning to Cleveland unscathed, Hanna had more pertinent opinions to cultivate than those of Oliver Payne. He was described at the time by one of his officers as "full-faced, with side whiskers; full-chested, square-shouldered; in fact a very manly man and thoroughly conscientious in the discharge of his duties."[8] That may have vanquished Charlotte Augusta Rhodes, but evidently it wasn't enough to overcome the prejudices of Hanna's future father-in-law, the redoubtable Daniel P. Rhodes. Raised in Vermont, Rhodes had moved to Cleveland by the age of thirty, made his fortune in coal and railroads, and by the time of the Civil War was moving into iron manufacturing. A pillar of St. John's Episcopal Church in the former Ohio City, he lived in Franklin Circle, the most fashionable address on the West Side. More to the point, however, Rhodes was a staunch Democrat distantly related to the late Stephen A. Douglas. "I like you very well, Mark," he would tell his daughter's Republican suitor, "but you are a damned

Charlotte Rhodes wed Marcus Hanna in the family parish, St. John's Episcopal Church, in Ohio City. Now Cleveland's oldest standing church building, St. John's was dedicated in 1838 and is said to have been an important station on the underground railroad. From the tower, escaping slaves could watch for signals from ships on Lake Erie that would convey them to Canada. The Hannas remained parishioners at St. John's until the senator's death in 1904.

Samuel Andrews, a young English mechanic, was the catalyst that got commission merchants Maurice Clark and John D. Rockefeller involved in oil refining. Though his support enabled Rockefeller to acquire the business from Clark and his brothers, Andrews later sold his interest in the resultant Standard Oil for $1 million. He spent much of it on a hundred-room castellated mansion on Euclid Avenue known as "Andrews' Folly."

screecher for freedom."[9] Love eventually had its way, and Charlotte Rhodes became Mrs. Marcus A. Hanna at St. John's in the fall of 1864. Even then the elder Rhodes took a while to mellow, disparaging Mark's independent business pursuits and urging him to join his iron business. Eventually Hanna succumbed, and in time Rhodes & Company would be known throughout the Great Lakes iron industry as M. A. Hanna & Company.

John D. Rockefeller's path to success led through an industry that barely existed in 1861. The coming of war brought a business boom that launched Clark & Rockefeller on a prosperous beginning as commission merchants. By 1863 they had quadrupled their quarters, taking the next three adjacent offices on River

Street. Among their incoming consignments, the partners began to notice increasing amounts of crude oil shipments. On August 28, 1859, during the months between the formation of Clark & Rockefeller and John Brown's raid at Harpers Ferry, Col. Edwin Drake brought in the world's first oil well, in western Pennsylvania. According to some accounts, Rockefeller himself went at the behest of several Cleveland businessmen for a personal inspection of the oil regions.[10] More certain is the role of a young Englishman named Samuel Andrews, who had come to Cleveland in 1857 and found employment as a mechanic in a lard-oil refinery. He took his idea for starting a petroleum refinery to Clark & Rockefeller, and soon the three were developing their plans at breakfast meetings at Rockefeller's home on Cheshire Street.

The upshot of these sessions was the formation in 1863 of a new oil refining firm, Andrews, Clark & Company. Rockefeller was a silent partner in the beginning, neither he nor Maurice Clark quitting their day jobs with the commission business as yet. John D. played an active role behind the scenes, however, being instrumental in acquiring for the new company's refinery a three-acre parcel of land on Kingsbury Run, a tributary feeding into the Cuyahoga River a couple of miles south of its mouth. As the Excelsior Oil Works, it spread over 100 acres and fulfilled Edwin Cowles's vision of the Cuyahoga as an industrial river. Rockefeller himself was often on the grounds, not only overseeing operations but lending a hand physically when necessary. Besides its access to the river, another advantage of the site was its proximity to the new Atlantic & Great Western Railroad, soon to become the nation's chief oil carrier. "It was a piece of luck for Cleveland that the oil fields were first tapped near their northwestern border, and not to the south near Pittsburgh," wrote Rockefeller's biographer, Allan Nevins. "It was a far greater piece of luck that this new railroad, planned without thought of oil, so quickly furnished cheap communication with the wells."[11]

With a thriving grocery business on the one hand and a stake in a promising new industry on the other, the young entrepreneur was ready to take another major step in his life. One of Rockefeller's classmates at Central High School had been a girl named Laura Celestia Spelman, whose home had been rumored to be an underground railroad station for fugitive slaves. Although John D. dropped out to go into business, "Cettie" graduated and went on to teach at Cleveland Institute, in the old Cleveland University building in University Heights. Rockefeller did not attend to business so closely as to neglect his acquaintance with the young teacher, and their friendship led to courtship and finally, on September 8, 1864, to marriage. It happened to be only three weeks prior to the marriage of their old Central High schoolmate, Mark Hanna, to Charlotte Rhodes. In another curious parallel, Hanna at the time also happened to be involved in the oil business, though with far different results. Father-in-law Rhodes had no faith in the fledgling industry and would respond to every fire bell he heard with the

One of Cleveland's leading businessmen was William Bingham, who began his career in hardware and later became involved in banking, manufacturing, and railroads. He backed the Union war effort by helping to raise volunteers and provide relief funds for their families.

gloomy observation, "There! I suppose Mark's damned oil refinery is burning down."[12] Eventually it became a self-fulfilling prophecy, which was the decisive factor in diverting Hanna from oil into iron.

Rockefeller's oil venture prospered to the point where he felt secure enough to quit the produce business in order to give the new industry his full attention. Fresh fields were opening in Pennsylvania, and the boom was heard and felt in Cleveland. There were some thirty refineries in the city, all of them small-scale operations employing a dozen or two workers. Rockefeller wanted to expand, but his conservative partners, namely Maurice Clark and his two brothers, balked. Securing the support of Samuel Andrews, Rockefeller forced a showdown and bought out the Clarks for $72,500. On May 24, 1865, six weeks after Lee's surrender at Appomattox, the *Leader* announced the formation of "Rockefeller and Andrews, Excelsior Oil Works." By November 1 Rockefeller and Andrews was credited with having paid the largest single tax ever collected in the Cleveland district, a sum of $31,800.[13] Known now as the Standard works, the operation was easily the city's leading refinery and stood poised for even greater conquests.

It proved to be much more than "business as usual" in Cleveland during the Civil War. Another masculine monopoly of the times—politics—was also in a state of transition. The Republican national platform in 1860 had bid for the support of the business interests of the old Whig Party with planks advocating internal improvements, a Pacific railroad, liberal immigration policies, and a protective tariff. But the party had been originally founded in 1854 on the antislavery feeling of the North, an issue thrust to the forefront by the onset of the Civil War. For the radical core of the party, slavery became more than ever the first order of business.

As the Western Reserve was the antislavery heart of Ohio, so Ashtabula County was the radical stronghold of the Reserve and the political base of Joshua R. Giddings, one of the first antislavery members of Congress, who had recently been appointed U.S. consul-general to Canada. From Montreal he wrote to senator Charles Sumner of Massachusetts, "The first gun fired at Fort Sumter rang out the death-knell of slavery."[14] The Republican spokesman in Ashtabula County was William Cooper Howells, editor of the *Sentinel*. His son, William Dean, had been rewarded for his campaign biography of Lincoln with the consulship at Venice, which proved a splendid vantage point from which to view the ensuing conflict. "The war has begun," the elder Howells editorialized on April 17, 1861, "the result will be universal Freedom or Slavery." A month later, the Grand River Congregational Conference resolved that "a speedy proclamation should be heard, 'proclaiming liberty throughout all the land to all the inhabitants thereof.'"[15]

Cleveland Republicans, however, received a shock in the local elections in

This collection of nondescript shacks in Kingsbury Run was destined to grow into the world's largest oil company. It was established as the Excelsior Works in 1863 by John D. Rockefeller, who would reorganize it in 1870 as Standard Oil. Kingsbury Run gave the fledgling refinery access to both the Cuyahoga River and the Atlantic & Great Western Railroad.

the spring of 1861. Running under a "Union-Democratic" ticket, the opposition elected a mayor by 700 votes. The tactic also proved successful for Democrats in Sandusky, Toledo, Columbus, and Cincinnati. The lesson was not wasted on Ohio Republicans, who co-opted the Union label for the state elections in the fall. Declining to call a Republican convention, the Republican State Central Nominating Committee instead invited Democrats to join them in a Union nominating convention. Some responded, but the outflanked Democratic State Central Committee decided to run a regular Democratic ticket. Radical Republicans might have liked to do the same but had little choice except to follow party leaders into the Union movement. The Union convention proceeded to write a state platform incorporating the Crittenden Resolution, which had been passed by the U.S. Congress, pledging that the war was being waged to preserve the Union and not to interfere with slavery. For governor they nominated a prowar Democrat, David Tod of Youngstown, who defeated the regular Democratic candidate by 50,000 votes.

Originally a silent partner, dynamic young John D. Rockefeller became the dominant force behind the rise of the refining firm of Andrews, Clark & Co. It was Rockefeller who acquired the site and supervised the construction of the company's Excelsior Works in Kingsbury Run. In 1864 the future tycoon laid aside busine ss long enough to marry a former classmate at Central High, Miss Laura Spelman.

Meanwhile, the logic of war managed to keep the slavery issue very much alive. Slaves escaping across Union lines were considered "contraband of war" by some Union generals, who refused to return them to their owners. Col. Rutherford B. Hayes wrote from West Virginia in 1861 to an uncle in Fremont, Ohio, asking him to find employment for a family of contrabands who had departed for the state.[16] After Congress the following year forbade Union officers from using their forces to capture fugitives, Brig. Gen. James A. Garfield refused to obey a commanding officer who ordered the camp searched for fugitives, telling him that if generals wished to disobey an act of Congress "they must do it themselves."[17] Congress continued to chip away at slavery where it constitutionally could throughout 1862, abolishing it in the territories and Washington, D.C., and declaring slaves used in the rebellion or the property of rebels to be subject to confiscation.

Still, the government failed to keep up with radical sentiment. In a single week in Ashtabula County in November 1861, antislavery meetings were scheduled for six different nights in six different townships. Petitions were circulated and signed, citing slavery as "the original and real cause of the present rebellion" and calling on Congress to abolish it and accept "able-bodied colored men . . . as volunteers to aid us in arms."[18] When the conservative Republican organ in Columbus, the *Ohio State Journal,* expressed reservations about the wisdom of emancipation, the *Ashtabula Sentinel* answered forcibly, "But are you prepared to shed the blood of the free white men of the North so needlessly, as the protracting of this war will do? . . . The military necessity demands any just means to shorten the war a single day." At that point in the war, every day hundreds of men were dying, and the government was going another $1.5 million into debt. "The right of the Government to emancipate the Slaves, has been established beyond cavil by John Quincy Adams and others. . . . But remember: a single life unnecessarily sacrificed, is to be answered for by those who protract the war when it can be honorably closed."[19] Only slightly less frenetically, the *Cleveland Leader* joined in the radical chorus. "Slavery is the cause of this war, and while the war lasts the cause will come up," wrote Edwin Cowles. "Let our national representatives meet the issue fearlessly and prescribe for it boldly."[20]

Democrats responded to these demands with an initiative campaign of their own. The Achilles' heel of the emancipation movement was racism, and another petition drive soon arose demanding that the state legislature enact laws prohibiting the further immigration of African Americans into Ohio. It centered in the southern half of the state, where it was fanned by *The Crisis,* an ultraconservative Democratic weekly edited in Columbus by Samuel Medary. A sample form printed in that journal on December 3, 1862, opened with the dire prediction that "events are occurring which will—unless restrained—cast upon the free State of Ohio, a large number of negroes and mulattoes; increasing thereby a grievance, with which the people are already heavily burdened, and which we believe

Many of Cleveland's emerging millionaires in the boom years following the Civil War announced their arrival in the upper classes by building mansions on the prestigious Euclid Avenue. "There is one street called Euclid Street," wrote an English visitor, "which for its beauty, its leafy trees, its well-built villas, its aspect, and its cleanly condition, would be worthy of Paris . . . or of Berlin." Among the nameplates on "Millionaires' Row" were those of Amasa Stone, Samuel Andrews, John D. Rockefeller, and John Hay.

War Democrat John Brough of Marietta defeated the antiwar Clement Vallandigham for governor of Ohio in 1863. "Ohio has saved the Nation," exclaimed President Lincoln at the news. As governor, Brough was instrumental in the enlisting of 85,000 Northern volunteers to provide behind-the-lines support for Gen. U. S. Grant's army during the Wilderness campaign.

would eventually become an unbearable one; thereby causing results unpleasant to the white population and dangerous to the colored." Part of a larger movement sweeping the Old Northwest, the agitation soon produced actual exclusion acts or proposals in Indiana, Illinois, and Iowa, leading Democratic Cassandras to warn against Ohio becoming a "dumping-ground" for freed slaves. By May *The Crisis* estimated that 40,000 Ohioans had signed exclusion petitions. There were outbreaks of racial violence that summer in Cincinnati and Toledo.

Following Charles Farrar Browne's (a.k.a., Artemus Ward) departure from Cleveland in 1860, an able successor appeared in northwest Ohio in the person of David Ross Locke. Writing as "Petroleum V. Nasby" for the *Hancock Jeffersonian* in Findlay, Locke aimed an acid-tipped pen at the exclusion campaign balloon. "There is now fifteen niggers, men, wimin, and childern, or ruther, mail, femail, and yung, in Wingert's Corners, and yisterday another arrove," bewailed Nasby. At that rate they would attain a majority in Locke's fictitious town in another sixty years "and may, ef they git mean enuff, tyrannize over us, even ez we air tyrannizin over them." Nasby therefore proposed a mass meeting to consider the following:

> *Resolved,* That the niggers be druv out uv Wingert's Corners, and that sich property ez they may hev accumulatid be confiscatid. . . .
> *Resolved,* That the ablishnists who oppose these resolushens all want to marry a nigger.
> *Resolved,* That Dr. Petts, in rentin a part uv his bildin to niggers, hez struck a blow at the very foundashuns uv sosiety.

"Our harths is in danger!" warned Nasby in his peroration, closing with the slogan "Ameriky for white men!"[21]

Unfortunately, political life in Ohio that fall was imitating Locke's satirical art. Democrats in central Ohio were campaigning under the slogan of "the Union as it was, the Constitution as it is, and the niggers where they are."[22] Within a week of the Battle of Antietam—but only three weeks before the elections—Lincoln issued the Preliminary Emancipation Proclamation. In Cleveland the *Plain Dealer,* though it still carried the Union ticket under its masthead, nevertheless printed the opposition slate at the bottom of the page "for the benefit of those of our Democratic readers who do not unite with the Union movement."[23] Democrats swept Ohio in October, winning state offices by an average of 5,000 votes and electing fourteen of the state's nineteen U.S. congressmen. There were similar Democratic gains in Indiana, Illinois, and other Northern states. A rare bright spot in Ohio was the election to Congress of rising Republican star James A. Garfield, who carried the Ashtabula district by nearly 7,000 votes without even campaigning. In the Cleveland district the Union ticket had dropped the ultraradical A. G. Riddle in favor of Rufus Spalding, defender of the Oberlin Rescuers and Sara Bagby, who likewise won election. Most of the Union-Republican losses had occurred in the southeastern counties along the Ohio River, where the fears of black migration presumably were greatest.

One result of the Democratic gains was the return of the *Plain Dealer* to party regularity on the ground that Lincoln had surrendered to the radicals.[24] The Democratic *Cincinnati Enquirer* read the returns as a mandate for Lincoln to rescind the Emancipation Proclamation, a possibility actually feared by many radicals.[25] The president held firmly to his course, however. None of the areas in rebellion having laid down their arms in the hundred days following his Prelimi-

HON. CLEMENT L. VALLANDIGHAM.
Page 315.

Long before Eugene V. Debs ran for president from a prison cell, Clement L. Vallandigham ran for governor of Ohio from political exile in Canada. The *Dayton Democrat* had been sentenced to imprisonment by military authorities for an antiwar speech, but President Lincoln commuted his sentence to banishment to the Confederacy, from where Vallandigham made his way to Windsor and the Democratic gubernatorial nomination. Practicing law after the war, he died of an accidental, self-inflicted gunshot wound sustained while demonstrating his theory of how a murder had actually occurred.

nary Proclamation, Lincoln signed the final Emancipation Proclamation on New Year's Day 1863, declaring all slaves in the territories still held by rebel forces to be "forever free."

THE CAMPAIGN OF 1856.

FREMONT SONGS
FOR THE PEOPLE,
ORIGINAL AND SELECTED.

J. C. FREMONT.

COMPILED BY THOMAS DREW,
EDITOR OF THE MASSACHUSETTS SPY.

BOSTON:
PUBLISHED BY JOHN P. JEWETT AND COMPANY.
CLEVELAND, OHIO:
JEWETT, PROCTOR AND WORTHINGTON.
NEW YORK: SHELDON, BLAKEMAN AND COMPANY.
1856.

A splinter group of radical Republicans gathered in Cleveland early in 1864 to nominate John Frémont for president. Though Clevelanders overwhelmingly favored the renomination of Abraham Lincoln, they were flattered to be hosting the city's first national political convention. Frémont, who had been the Republicans' first presidential candidate in 1856, bowed to reality and withdrew from the 1864 contest.

"All hail then to the Proclamation," trumpeted the *Cleveland Leader,* "a magnificent stride in the march of human national progress toward the day of Universal Love and Brotherhood."[26] Naturally the *Ashtabula Sentinel* joined in approbation, though not without a quibble. "We could have wished that it had been based upon the intrinsic justice of emancipation, and not offered as a military necessity," wrote W. C. Howells.[27] But no equivocation whatsoever could be detected in Samuel Medary's condemnation of the Proclamation, as brayed forth by a three-column head in *The Crisis:*

> The Deed is Done!
> The Dictator presumes to Speak!
> The Negro in the Ascendant!

Straining to give expression to his contempt, Medary summarized the long-dreaded proclamation as the culminating folly of the "half-witted usurper" and his "fanatical and brainless followers."[28]

Indeed, Ohio Democrats would proceed to overplay their contumacy in 1863. Maj. Gen. Ambrose E. Burnside, commander of the Military Department of the Ohio in Cincinnati, had issued an order against "the habit of declaring sympathies for the enemy." It was challenged by former Democratic congressman Clement L. Vallandigham of Dayton, who delivered an address in Mt. Vernon denouncing "Lincoln and his minions" for "the attempts now being made to build up a monarchy upon the ruins of a free government." Arrested by Burnside and tried by a military commission, Vallandigham was found guilty and sentenced to imprisonment, a punishment commuted by Lincoln to banishment to the Confederacy. Things then really got interesting when the Democratic state convention in Columbus nominated the exiled politician in absentia for governor of Ohio. Vallandigham made his way through the South and the Northern blockade to Canada, where he accepted the nomination and prepared to run his peace campaign from Windsor, Ontario.

Ohio Republicans continued to subordinate their partisanship to the Union movement. Though Governor Tod had been deemed too lukewarm in his acceptance of the Emancipation Proclamation, the Union convention nominated for governor another prowar Democrat, John Brough of Marietta. The Union platform avoided a statement on emancipation but pledged support to Lincoln in his prosecution of the war. They succeeded thereby in retaining the support of those Democrats in favor of suppressing the rebellion. "I was very glad to learn that Father [H. B. Payne] had taken a stand against Vallandigham & Co.," wrote Democrat Oliver Payne to his brother from the field in Tennessee.[29] (Under a bill recently enacted by the state legislature, Ohio soldiers would be able to vote from the field in this election.) As an indication of how important this state contest was regarded by Washington, Secretary of the Treasury Salmon P. Chase was urging his fellow Ohioans in the Federal bureaucracy to go home and vote. They needn't have taken the trouble, as Brough buried Vallandigham by a wide margin of 100,000 votes, 40,000 of which had come from Ohio troops. "Glory to God in the highest" cried Lincoln as the returns were received in Washington, "Ohio has saved the Nation."

In fact, the chief challenges to Lincoln's reelection the following year in Ohio came not from Democrats but from within his own party. As the national party made plans to run a Union campaign in 1864, the radical wing of the Republicans displayed signs of rebellion. First came a "Chase boom," in which radicals conspired to replace Lincoln on the ticket with his Secretary of the Treasury. Several Ohioans were prominent in this movement, including U.S. congressmen James Garfield and James Ashley and U.S. senators Benjamin F. Wade and (less enthusiastically) John Sherman. An "Organization to make S. P. Chase President" issued a pair of anti-Lincoln tracts, which had the unintended consequence of rallying support behind the president. After Union caucuses in the Ohio and Indiana legislatures delivered endorsements of Lincoln, Chase publicly withdrew his name from consideration in March.

Two months later another group of dissident Republicans convened in Cleveland. Dominated by radical Germans, they were supporters of Gen. John Frémont, the Republican standard-bearer in 1856. Frémont had been the darling of the radicals ever since issuing a proclamation in 1861 freeing slaves under his former command in Missouri, a premature gesture rescinded by Lincoln as commander in chief. Nearly half of the delegates to Cleveland came from Missouri, in fact, with most of the remainder from Illinois, New York, and Pennsylvania. Clevelanders seemed to take little interest in the proceedings but considerable pride in hosting their first national political convention. Calling it the "sorehead" convention, the *Leader* observed, "In view of the fact that the soundest anti-slavery men of the nation are in favor of Mr. Lincoln's renomination, it little becomes the malcontents who are to meet in this city to prate about a more radical anti-slavery policy."[30] They went ahead, nonetheless, to nominate Frémont by acclamation, though the nominee would withdraw from the race in September.

Union-Republicans met in Baltimore in May to nominate Abraham Lincoln for president with Andrew Johnson of Tennessee as his running mate. Party radicals could take satisfaction in the platform's call for a constitutional amendment to end slavery. Trying to have it both ways, the Democrats nominated Gen. George B. McClellan for president on a platform calling for peace. They posed enough of a threat to cause Lincoln serious worry, at least until Union military victories in the fall knocked the supports out from under their platform. As Garfield wrote his wife in September, Gen. Phil Sheridan was making a more powerful political speech with his Shenandoah Valley campaign than all the stump-speakers at

Both candidates could claim to be in favor of the Union in the presidential election of 1864. While the Republican Abraham Lincoln came out for "Union and Liberty" as the Great Emancipator, however, the Democrat George B. McClellan took the more conservative stance of "the Union and the Constitution." Thanks to Northern military victories during the campaign, Lincoln carried both Ohio and the election.

home.[31] Lincoln carried Ohio by 60,000 votes in November, and the Union-Republicans captured 17 of the state's 19 congressional seats.

Racial relations in Ohio also showed signs of recovery from their low state in 1862. A second colored regiment was authorized to be filled in the state early in 1864, and by the end of the war more than 5,000 colored troops had been raised in Ohio. A considerable number were contrabands or freedmen just up from the former slave states. Black citizens were invited to participate in Union victory celebrations even in Cincinnati. In Cleveland the ejection of the wife of a Negro soldier from a streetcar had sparked civic outrage resulting in an order that blacks be admitted on all cars.[32] (The *Leader* noted with satisfaction the distress experienced weeks after the war by two visiting Texans in a Cleveland restaurant, when two Negroes were seated at an adjoining table.[33]) Meeting in Xenia early in 1865, the Convention of the Colored Men of Ohio had expressed gratification over the imminent demise of chattel slavery but went on to call for an end to the continuing slavery of racial discrimination laws. The Ohio Legislature did its part by nullifying the last of the state's remaining "Black Laws" with a new statute making establishment of a year's residence in a township the sole qualification for poor relief.

Finally, it was Ohio congressman James M. Ashley of Toledo who, on December 14, 1863, introduced in Congress the Thirteenth Amendment, ending slavery. Although passed easily in the Senate, it encountered more resistance in the House of Representatives due to the Democratic gains made in Ohio and other states in 1862. Petitions for passage were circulated during Cleveland's Northern Ohio Sanitary Fair in the winter of 1864, but the Union victories in the fall elections that year probably exerted more practical influence. During the ensuing lame duck session of Congress, eight Democratic abstentions finally released the Thirteenth Amendment to the states for ratification. Governor John Brough submitted it with his endorsement to the Ohio Legislature, where it was speedily approved by a party vote of 58-12 in the House of Representatives and by a margin of 20-4 in the Ohio Senate.

While most of the nation's attention had been focused on the slavery issue, a quieter revolution had been going on in the bureaucracies of the Federal government. A new war hero took his place alongside such Northern commanders as Grant, Sherman, Thomas, and Sheridan: Quartermaster General Montgomery C. Meigs. As the North's chief procurement officer, Meigs spent $1.5 billion—half the direct cost of the conflict—during the four years of the Civil War. Though at first he tried to spread his orders as broadly as possible among firms of all sizes, the demands of the Northern war machine increasingly led him to favor the larger, more efficient enterprises, thereby providing the model for the emerging big business of the ensuing Gilded Age. One of the changes brought about by the organization of the war effort involved the standardization of railroad gauges. As many as eight different gauges were in use before the war, but with the passage of the Pacific Railway Act of 1862 the 4-foot-8½-inch Stephenson gauge of England emerged as the American standard. Other changes included the standardization of railroad time and the furnishment of standard male sizes by the government to provide suppliers with uniforms.

One government innovation that in time would become one of its most visibly pervasive activities was extensively pioneered in Cleveland during the Civil War. It occurred in the post office, which had not yet acquired its reputation for reliability. Home mail delivery was an unheard-of luxury, unless one was wealthy enough to be able to afford the expensive services of a private, or "mercenary" carrier. The office of local postmaster was not a civil service position but rather a political plum, generally doled out to editors of the newspapers supporting the national party in power, who, for the most part, served as part-time postmasters, content to collect the emoluments of office while leaving postal operations to the full-time clerks. (And accidents did happen, sometimes involving the disappearance of bundles of a rival newspaper from the office before subscribers could call for them.)

With the election of Abraham Lincoln, Edwin Cowles, editor of the *Leader,* became postmaster in Cleveland. While never accused of misplacing opposition newspapers, he evidently became more of a hands-on postmaster than the average. One of his clerks was a fifty-year-old former harness maker named Joseph W. Briggs. Observing Clevelanders queued up for their mail during the holiday season of 1862, Briggs, who had once patented a stitching machine, figured there had to be a better way. He took his idea for free home delivery to Postmaster Cowles, whose interest was piqued by the thought of getting Editor Cowles's *Leader* directly into the hands of its readers. Cowles passed the proposal on to Postmaster General Montgomery Blair in Washington, who got enabling legislation passed by Congress on March 3, 1863.[34]

Cleveland's first U.S. Post Office was built on the east side of Public Square in 1858. Sara Lucy Bagby was detained there during her fugitive slave hearing in 1861, and it was there that Joseph W. Briggs worked out the details of free home delivery of mail during the Civil War. The Italian renaissance building was replaced on the same site in 1910 by the present Howard M. Metzembaum Federal Courthouse.

POST OFFICE AND CUSTOM HOUSE.

Outside of Cleveland, it did not appear at first to be an idea the country was waiting for. Postmaster Cowles and clerk Briggs, however, were ready to begin the experiment on July 1, 1863, the first day the law went into effect.[35] Briggs became one of the first three carriers, to be identified by pink bands on their hats bearing the inscription "Post Office Letter Carrier." (Later he would receive credit for helping to design the first letter carrier's uniform.) His initial route extended from the Cuyahoga River to Erie (East 9th) Street, and from the lake down to University Heights (today's Tremont). Inevitably there were snags to be ironed out. "The Letter Carriers experience great difficulty in ascertaining the residences of people to whom letters are directed, owing to the fact that the street and number are not written in addition to the direction on the letters," stated the *Leader* after five weeks, urging people to provide correspondents with their full addresses.[36] Many houses lacked numbers; streets needed signs or even names. Briggs was said to have discovered two Lincoln Streets on his route, a problem solved Solomon-fashion by getting one renamed Abraham Street.

Inventor that he was, Briggs kept coming up with ways to fine-tune the new system. When he forwarded some suggestions to Washington in 1864, Postmaster General Blair reputedly exclaimed, "Here is the man I want," and appointed Briggs as a special agent to help implement home delivery nationwide. The Clevelander spent a good part of the remainder of his life on the road as a sort of traveling trouble-shooter. The last weeks of the war, for example, saw him in Buffalo, where he wrote his wife, Harmony, that he found "things in such a shape that I deem it best for me to make tracks for Washington. I go to advise with the Department in regard to the better plan to make the carrier system more perfect and advantageous to the Dept. and the country."[37] By the time of his death in 1872—from overwork, it was said—Briggs had helped organize free delivery in more than fifty cities, coast to coast.

Clevelanders took to the innovation from the beginning. This was especially true of the business community, which benefitted from five deliveries daily. On the eve of its first anniversary, the *Leader* printed an endorsement of the "Free Delivery System" signed by nearly a hundred local businessmen and industrialists. "So far our letters have been delivered correctly, promptly, and more frequently than we have heretofore been in the habit of calling at the office," read their card. "We would advise all who are not having their letters delivered at their places of business or residences, to try the new system, not doubting that it will prove eminently satisfactory." Among the satisfied clients were Robert Hanna & Company, Clark & Rockefeller, S. Brainard & Company, and the Cleveland Rolling Mill.[38]

Improved mail service wasn't the only thing the government was prepared to do for business. In the absence of Southern Democrats, as a consequence of secession, Congress proceeded to enact the economic planks of the Republican platform, including a Pacific Railway Act to subsidize a transcontinental railroad and

An unsuccessful inventor working as a clerk in the Cleveland branch of the U.S. Post Office, Joseph W. Briggs is credited with conceiving the idea of free home delivery of mail. Briggs spent the remainder of his life traveling to help inaugurate the new system in other American cities.

the highest tariff duties since 1828 for the encouragement of domestic industry. Cleveland businessmen were determined to capture their share of the anticipated expansion. Early in 1866 the Board of Trade issued its first *Annual Statement of the Trade, Commerce and Manufactures of the City of Cleveland*. "At Cleveland," it observed, "the products of the coal fields meet the rich iron and copper ores from Lake Superior, making it the cheapest possible point for the manufacture of all articles in which these metals are used. No other city in the West, at least, can claim a tithe of the advantages in this respect, which Cleveland justly and undeniably possesses." With "well directed enterprise," concluded the report, it was Cleveland's destiny "to stand in the front rank of manufacturing cities of the Union."[39]

Returning Civil War veterans, then, particularly those of general officer rank, would find peacetime career opportunities in business as well as politics. Those who chose the more traditional political route famously included Generals Rutherford B. Hayes and James A. Garfield. Gen. Mortimer D. Leggett played both fields, serving as President Grant's commissioner of patents before returning to Cleveland to become one of the founders of the Brush Electric Company. Col. Oliver Hazard Payne returned directly to Cleveland to enter the effervescent oil industry. His firm of Clark, Payne & Company became the principal local competition of Rockefeller's concern. When Rockefeller invited Payne to merge his operation with Standard Oil in 1872, Payne was one of those Clevelanders astute enough to accept Standard stock in lieu of cash. He would eventually leave an estate valued at $190 million.

Return to the Square

IT STARTED OUT AS A QUIET GOOD FRIDAY evening at home for Albert G. Riddle, the former Cleveland congressman now practicing law in Washington, D.C. While his eldest daughter had gone out on a theater date (despite it's being Good Friday!), Riddle remained at home with his wife, younger children, and a couple of friends. At 9:00 they heard footsteps hurrying up the stairs, and in burst a pale and wild-eyed Florence Riddle, followed by her escort.

"O Father!" she gasped, "Wilkes Booth has shot the President. He leaped down upon the stage and rushed back, and immediately a tall man from the crowd rushed after him." They had been to Ford's Theatre to see Laura Keene in *Our American Cousin* and had witnessed the assassination of Abraham Lincoln.

Feeling the "savage old spirit to kill" coming on him once again, Riddle grabbed his Remingtons (undoubtedly the same weapons he had taken four years before to the first Battle of Bull Run) and dashed out into the street. "Already there was a murmur of excited voices, and a shiver of fright all through the city," he later recalled. Making his way toward Secretary of War Edwin Stanton's house on K Street, Riddle heard the "thousand-tongued rumor" circulating about additional assassination attempts against the vice president and other cabinet members. As he continued on to the residence of Secretary of State William H. Seward, the only other government official actually attacked, though not mortally, that evening, the "nature and extent of the conspiracy" began to take on clearer outlines. In vigilante fashion, he and others agreed to disperse to various sections of the city to look for any likely perpetrators. "I patrolled the boundary from 14th to 7th streets; luckily no suspicious-looking person met my eyes, and the revolvers were not taken out of their places," he concluded.[1]

Frank Rieley was in Nashville waiting to be mustered out of the cavalry when he heard the news. "That was a sad thing the death of the President, but it cannot be helped now," he wrote his mother in Cleveland two days later. Nashville

Actor John Wilkes Booth assassinated president Abraham Lincoln in Ford's Theatre, breaking his leg as he jumped from the presidential box to the stage in making his escape. Two weeks later he was trapped and killed in a Virginia barn by Union troops. He was the younger brother of Edwin Booth, the foremost tragedian of the American stage.

had been preparing to celebrate the end of the war on April 15, but "before they had fairly got started, the news came of the president being killed, and every face which looked bright and joyous before turned to sadness."[2]

In Cleveland Edwin Cowles inverted the column rules of the *Leader*'s front page on April 15, 1865, to form a heavy black border for the banks of shocking headlines:

ASSASSINATION!
OF PRESIDENT LINCOLN!!!
He Is Shot Through the Head, While in the Theater
Wound Pronounced Mortal!
SECRETARY SEWARD also Assassinated!!
ESCAPE OF THE ASSASSIN

"How shall we write the terrible words that we must record to-night!" wrote Cowles. "The brain reels, the heart sickens, the whole frame shudders at the very thought of our great affliction." Like Frank Rieley, Cowles dwelled on the ironic contrast between the recent mood of triumph and thanksgiving over the end of the long war and the sudden plunge into grief and despair over the loss of "our patriotic, self-sacrificing, devoted and now martyred President." In a sentence that boded ill for Lincoln's hopes for a lenient Reconstruction, the editor vowed, "Over his murdered cor[p]se every lover of the Union will swear eternal vengeance upon treason and traitors."[3] The *Leader* called for a meeting "to give expression to the public grief" that afternoon on Public Square, an idea that received official sanction later that morning in a proclamation issued by mayor George B. Senter. The anti-Lincoln *Plain Dealer* was mercifully spared the problem of how to play the story. In steep decline due to its Copperhead policies, it had temporarily suspended publication early in March, after the widow of Joseph Gray petitioned the court to remove John Stephenson as administrator and force his resignation as editor. (While the Democratic paper struggled to reorganize, Republican wags had placed a white flag over its offices on hearing the news of the Confederate surrender at Appomattox.)

Like Albert Riddle in Washington, some Clevelanders responded to news of the assassination by succumbing to the vigilante impulse. Since they weren't likely to find any suspected assassins in northern Ohio, they turned their fury on the next best targets: traitors or perceived traitors at home. One such example was a visitor from southern Ohio, who heard about the assassination while being shaved at the Weddell House barbershop. "Lincoln was a d—d son of a b—h and ought to have been shot long ago," he was reported to have said. Chased out of the shop, he was pursued by a mob and badly beaten before being taken to the jail, presumably for protective custody.

AMUSEMENTS.

ACADEMY OF MUSIC.

NEXT TO ANGIER HOUSE, BANK ST.
JOHN ELLSLER, JR........Manager and Proprietor
JAS. DICKSON....................Stage Manager
C. BUSCH...........................Treasurer

PRICES OF ADMISSION—Boxes and Parquette, 50 cts
Family Circle, 25 cts; Gallery, 15 cts. ots reserved
during the day, 50 cts. Single seats Private Boxes
75 cts. Entire Box $2,00, $3,00, and $5,00.

SCHILLER! SCHILLER!!

The great German Poet.

Positively the Last Night of

J. WILKES BOOTH,

On this occasion he will appear in Schiller's great
Drama of

THE ROBBERS,

AS...................CHARLES DE MOOR.

This Saturday Evening, December 5th, 1863,

Will be presented Schiller's grand and powerful
Tragedy of

THE ROBBERS,

OR THE FOREST OF BOHEMIA.

Charles De Moor...................Mr. J. W. BOOTH
Amelia............................Mrs. Effie Ellsler
Francis De Moor.................Mr. Colin Stewart
Swetzer.........................Mr. J. C. McCollom
Spiegelberg.....................Mr. James Lewis

Mr. G. I. LESLIE, will make his first appearance
upon the stage, volunteering to recite Drake's celebrated address to the American Flag.

To conclude with the capital Farce called

MY NEIGHBOR'S WIFE.'

Mrs. Somerton................Mrs. James Dickson
Mr. Timothy Brown.............Mr. James Lewis

Monday evening, first appearance this season of
those favorite artists, Mr. and Mrs. F. B. CONWAY.

Doors open at 6¾ o'clock. Curtain will rise at 7½
o'clock

One of John Wilkes Booth's last professional stage appearances had been in late 1863 with John Ellsler's stock company at the Academy of Music in Cleveland. Besides *The Robbers*, Booth was also seen during this stand in two Shakespearean parts: the title role in *Richard III* and as Iago in *Othello*.

Not only were Cleveland's buildings draped in black, but many of her citizens wore somber accessories such as this badge of mourning for the wake of Abraham Lincoln in Cleveland. Estimates of the number that came to Cleveland to pay their respects from as far as Michigan and Pennsylvania ranged as high as 100,000.

For allegedly expressing his gratification over the news of Lincoln's assassination, Cleveland architect J. J. Husband was pursued by a mob and run out of town. Still not content, the outraged citizenry grabbed chisels and effaced the architect's name from the cornerstone of the Cuyahoga County Courthouse.

The most notorious local case of street justice involved the architect J. J. Husband, who had designed the Cuyahoga County Courthouse on Public Square. Seemingly a better architect than diplomat, he reportedly reacted to news of Lincoln's death by remarking to one mourner, "You have had your day of rejoicing, now I have mine." Remarks of a similar nature were alleged to have been heard by others. Husband himself appeared at the newspaper offices to deny that he had made any such comments, which would seem to indicate that he was either trying to rectify previous errors of judgment or quash unfounded rumors circulating around town. Whichever the case, it failed to mollify the angry mob that began to follow Husband back to his office over Fogg's store. Though he temporarily gave them the slip, the pursuers entered the building and finally cornered their prey on the roof. They first threw him through a skylight into his room and then went on to kick him out of his quarters and down the stairs to the street. There he was mercifully rescued by some "prominent citizens," who locked him up in his own courthouse for safekeeping. Husband managed to sneak off later in the day and exercised the good judgment of getting out of town. By nightfall his name had been chiseled from the cornerstone of the courthouse, and the architect was never again seen in the city. "Cleveland is an unhealthy place for traitors," commented the *Leader*.[4]

Tempers gradually cooled as Clevelanders turned to the somber duty of paying homage to the remains of Abraham Lincoln on their way back to Illinois. They had laid in state in the East Room of the White House, then in the Capitol

Rotunda, before being placed, on April 21, with the disinterred small casket of Lincoln's deceased son, Willie, on a special train for the long journey home. The funeral train reversed the convoluted route of Lincoln's progress to Washington four years earlier. It wound from Baltimore through Harrisburg and Philadelphia to New York, where George Bancroft gave an oration at Union Square. From there the lonesome train chugged mournfully up the Hudson Valley to Albany and then followed the Mohawk Valley to Buffalo and Erie. It was scheduled to arrive in Cleveland on April 28.

The Forest City greeted the appointed day dressed in black. "Not only the dwellings of the rich and the big business blocks thus wore the emblems of woe, but the houses of the poor, all bore some modest emblem of mourning," observed the *Leader*.[5] So great had been the demand for black bunting that many were obliged to dye their own. It rained that morning and throughout the day, causing many of the decorations to run and leave dark reminders of the occasion long afterward. All the city's hotels were filled. A delegation of 500, including two bands, had arrived from Detroit, while another 200 came from Meadville, Pennsylvania. People from the surrounding countryside jammed every road leading into the city that morning, causing the reception committee to leave nearly two hours in advance in order to meet the train on time.

As the nine-car funeral train approached the Union Depot on the Lake Shore line, it was greeted first by a tableau at Willson (East 55th) Street, where a young woman, identified only as Miss Fields, had set up an arbor of evergreens to frame her appearance as "the Goddess of Liberty in mourning."[6] Pulling into the depot shortly after seven o'clock, the train was then switched to the Cleveland & Pittsburgh line and drawn in reverse to the Euclid Street station, where a thirty-six-gun salute announced its arrival. Governor John Brough and his staff headed the Guard of Honor lined up to meet it. Among the civic pallbearers were David Tod, Henry B. Payne, and Amasa Stone. A military honor guard moved the coffin

Six white horses slowly pulled Lincoln's hearse down stately Euclid Street to the dirges of several bands and the hollow reports of a single cannon. Governor John Brough and former governor David Tod were among the six divisions of the funeral procession.

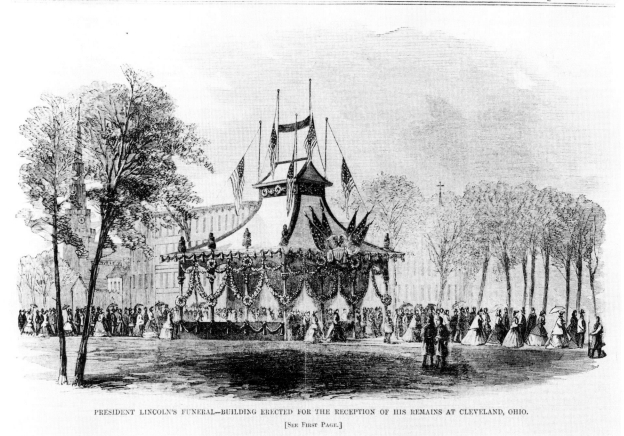

PRESIDENT LINCOLN'S FUNERAL—BUILDING ERECTED FOR THE RECEPTION OF HIS REMAINS AT CLEVELAND, OHIO.

[SEE FIRST PAGE.]

A special pavilion was erected on Public Square to shelter the wake of Abraham Lincoln in Cleveland. As depicted in *Harper's Weekly*, a double file of northern Ohio mourners moved past the open casket all day. Open umbrellas testify to the rain that persisted throughout the somber day and intensified in the evening during the return of the hearse to the lakefront depot for its journey to Illinois.

from the train to a hearse draped in black velvet with silver fringes and drawn by six white horses, each attended by a black groom. It proceeded down Euclid and was followed by a procession of dignitaries and civic groups organized into six divisions, the first of which was headed by Col. Oliver H. Payne as assistant marshall. Various bands sounded dirges, and a single cannon boomed on the half-hour as the marchers solemnly made their way to Public Square.

Finding no building in Cleveland large enough to accommodate the anticipated crowd, the Committee on Location of Remains opted to put up a special pavilion to shelter the president's corpse right in the Square, just east of the Perry Monument. A pagoda-like structure, twenty-four by thirty-six feet, it was open on the sides and covered with a white canvas roof that rose fourteen feet in height. A smaller belfry-like projection, which rose four feet above the center of the roof, was intended to form a canopy directly above the catafalque. Four black plumes rose above the eaves on either side of the building, which was further decorated with evergreen and floral wreathes and the national colors. Above the upper roof, a streamer bore the Latin inscription "*Extinctus amabitur idem*" ("Dead, he will be loved the same").

It was past nine o'clock when the coffin was placed on the catafalque and opened. Charles Pettit McIlvaine, bishop of the Diocese of Ohio, led some 10,000 mourners in prayer and intoned the Episcopal burial service. A *Herald* reporter found the appearance of the corpse "by no means satisfactory" to anyone familiar with the president's appearance in life and wrote frankly, "The color is leaden, almost brown; the forehead recedes sharp and clearly marked; the eyes deep sunk and close held upon the socket; the cheek bones, always high, are unusually prominent; the cheeks hollowed and deep pitted; the unnatural thin lips shut tight and firm as if glued together, and the small chin, covered with slig[h]t beard, seemed pointed and sharp."[7]

At ten o'clock the officials finally stepped aside, and the common people got their turn. Endlessly they filed past in a double column on either side of the coffin, at a steady rate of nearly 10,000 an hour. They entered from the east side of the Square, the head of the coffin being placed to the west. "The floor is so inclined that on entering the building the visitors will be able at once to see the remains and keep them in sight until nearly leaving the building," said the *Herald*. (Clevelanders were said to have delayed their visits until later in the day, giving out-of-towners a chance to pay their respects and catch evening trains home.) Mary Clark Brayton recalled, "Who of the thousands that passed, with downcast eye and muffled footfall, in review before that Silent Presence will ever forget the ineffable sadness of that day! The clouds dropping gentle rain, in sympathy with a nation's tears, the sighing wind lifting and swaying the draperies of the curtained pagoda . . . or the weird solemnities of the evening watch, when the moaning of the restless trees and the loud wail of the rising storm mingled fitfully with the wild strains of a dirge . . . as the bearers reverently raised their sacred burden, and the cortege, with nodding plumes and stately trappings, swept out into the dense darkness that fell like a pall upon the mournful scene."[8]

One who never forgot was Ella Grant Wilson, so small at the time that despite the tilt of the pagoda's floor, she was unable to see over the edge of the casket, even on tiptoe. A clean-shaven man with a high, broad forehead stepped up from the foot of the coffin. Lifting her up, he told her gently, "Little girl, there lies a great and good man. Never forget him." It was Salmon P. Chase, Lincoln's one-time rival for the Republican nomination, who served him and sometimes schemed against him as secretary of the Treasury, until Lincoln finally neutralized him by naming him chief justice of the Supreme Court.[9]

For twelve hours northern Ohioans continued to pass steadily through the funeral pagoda. Well past sunset, the casket was finally covered and removed from Public Square. It was taken directly to the lakefront depot via Superior and Vineyard Streets, accompanied, despite torrential rain and darkness, by an escort that included no fewer than three bands. More than 100,000 people had viewed Lincoln's remains, estimated the *Herald,* calling the total "much greater than ever

Accompanying the Lincoln funeral cortege through Ohio was Salmon P. Chase, chief justice of the U.S. Supreme Court. A former governor of Ohio, he had gone to Washington in 1861 to become Lincoln's secretary of the Treasury.

Some Ohio regiments raised their own Civil War memorabilia, such as this to the 7th Ohio Volunteer Infantry at Woodland Cemetery. The first Civil War regiment to be organized in Cleveland, the 7th saw action at Antietam, Chancellorsville, and Missionary Ridge.

before seen in Cleveland."[10] The *Leader* took care to note that "Messrs. J. Paige, of the New York Tribune, Dr. Adonis of the Chicago Tribune, N.H. Painter, of the Philadelphia Inquirer, C.R. Morgan and L.A. Gobright of the Associated Press" were among the visitors.[11] Presumably they weren't among the victims of the city's "light fingered fraternity," which worked the crowd despite the efforts of police to quarantine them beforehand. "Such things will happen in every great concourse of people, no matter how serious and solemn the occasion," commented the *Leader*. "The citizens of Cleveland and the visitors from other portions of Northern Ohio," concluded the *Herald*, "may well be proud of the admirable manner in which all the arrangements were carried out, the good order and decorum everywhere observed, and the deep spirit of respect to the memory of the great and good departed, which was universally manifested."[12]

It was over, but not forgotten. Lincoln himself had spoken at Gettysburg of the obligation of the living to "resolve that these dead shall not have died in vain." While he was thinking in terms of the unfinished Civil War, others, once the war was over, began to consider more material memorials for those who had fought on both sides. As might be expected, Civil War veterans were in the vanguard of the movement. Local units raised memorials to the 7th and the 23rd OVI at Woodland Cemetery, and the 103rd OVI established a reunion campground at Sheffield Lake. In 1879 a veterans' gathering at Case Hall proposed that a memorial monument for all the Civil War veterans of Cuyahoga County be erected in Public Square. Named to the committee of seven to expedite the plan were businessman William J. Gleason of the 150th OVI and architect Levi T. Scofield, who had once led a platoon of recruits to the office of John D. Rockefeller.

It proved to be a much longer campaign than the war it sought to memorialize. It was not until 1888 that the General Assembly passed enabling legislation authorizing the committee to proceed to raise funds and erect its monument on the southeast quadrant of Cleveland's Public Square. The original committee was expanded to a Soldiers' and Sailors' Monument Commission of twelve, including original members Gleason and Scofield. Among the newcomers was Maj. Gen. Mortimer D. Leggett. Donating his services as architect, Scofield went to work in a barn near East 9th and Euclid Avenue. He not only designed the monument itself but provided sketches for the statuary. Clay models were mocked up into full-sized wood and burlap skeletons in the studio before being sent out of state to be cast into bronze.

While Scofield and his assistants labored in the barn, a political battle over the monument was being waged outside. There happened to be a major obstacle standing in the way of the new monument's placement in its intended section of Public Square: the Perry Monument, which was dedicated with such pomp and ceremony on the eve of the Civil War. At the time, Perry's statue had been placed in the center of the Square, which was fenced off to traffic and designated as Monument Park. Since then, Public Square had been reopened to traffic and Perry moved into the desired southeast quadrant. There the commodore still found his champions, however, in the form of city parks officials who defended local

Chosen to design and execute the Cuyahoga County Soldiers' and Sailors' Monument was Capt. Levi T. Scofield, a Civil War veteran and architect. Other works by Scofield, who worked gratis on the monument, are the Scofield Building at East 9th and Euclid in downtown Cleveland and the Ohio State Reformatory in Mansfield.

It took years of lobbying
and litigation before Levi
Scofield could begin actual
construction of the Soldiers'
and Sailors' Monument
in 1892. Much of the
controversy centered around
the monument's proposed
location on the southeast
quadrant of Public Square,
necessitating the removal of
the Perry Monument, which
had been moved to that spot
after the Civil War.

prerogatives by taking Scofield to court. It took more than a year before the Ohio
Supreme Court broke the impasse by deciding that ownership of Public Square
was vested in the general public rather than the city, which meant that the Ohio
Legislature trumped Cleveland. Scofield thereupon moved onto the disputed site

by the end of 1892 and began digging foundations for his Civil War monument. As for the Perry Monument, it was resited in Wade Park, just the beginning of a long odyssey that has taken it to nearly as many ports as its seagoing namesake. A year and a half later, the Cuyahoga County Soldiers' and Sailors' Monument was ready for its own dedication on July 4, 1894.

Few who had attended the Perry dedication in 1860 would have recognized the Public Square of 1894. It was now the center of a city of 300,000, more than six times larger than the nascent metropolis of Civil War days. Among that expanded population were large contingents of nationalities scarcely heard of by the earlier Yankee-dominated population—Italians, Russians, Czechs, Poles, Slovaks, and Slovenes lured to the city's industries cradled during the Civil War. The city's black population had increased from a few hundred to several thousand, though the Great Migration from the South still lay in the future. Public Square itself mirrored the growing size and wealth of Cleveland. The Old Stone Church still stood opposite the northwest quadrant, but it was now overshadowed by two of the city's first skyscrapers, the massive ten-story Society for Savings Building and the elegant new Cuyahoga Building.

Dedication ceremonies for the new Civil War memorial were every bit as impressive as those for the Perry Monument thirty-four years earlier. By 10:00 A.M. the square was "filled to suffocation," in the words of the *Cleveland Press,* "and the windows of adjacent buildings were filled with admiring spectators."[13] They were welcomed by Ohio governor William McKinley, who would be the last Civil War

One of four heroic bronze groups cast from clay models for the exterior of the Soldiers' and Sailors' Monument was "The Color Guard." Dedicated to the infantry, it depicts an incident during the Battle of Resaca in which nine Union soldiers defended their regimental flag until everyone was either killed or wounded.

Then governor of Ohio, William McKinley of Canton spoke at the dedication of the Soldiers' and Sailors' Monument on July 4, 1894. McKinley had enlisted in the 23rd Ohio Volunteer Infantry as an eighteen-year-old private in 1861, rising to the rank of brevet major by the end of the war.

veteran to go to the White House. In a relatively brief address McKinley recalled the "hallowed memories" of what he still referred to as "Monumental Square," including the Perry dedication and the Lincoln obsequies as well as the more recent rites for another martyred president, Cleveland's James A. Garfield. Reflecting on the monument behind him, McKinley said, "It means sacrifice for the country we love. It means not only love of country but it means love of liberty, and, this alone would have inspired two millions, eight hundred thousand soldiers to leave home and family and fireside and to die if need be for our imperiled institutions."[14] Following the dedication a five-mile parade marched through the downtown, led by the Civil War veterans bearing their old battle flags.

Scofield's monument fully measured up to the pageantry of the occasion. A paragon of high Victorian style, it takes the form of an ornate stone base, forty feet square, out of which rises a 125-foot granite shaft—nearly as tall as the nearby Cuyahoga Building. Standing at the pinnacle is a fifteen-foot statue of Liberty, personified in the form of Scofield's wife, Elizabeth, who is said to have modeled for her husband wearing an old army overcoat. A broad esplanade surrounds the base, around which are placed four monumental sculpture groups representing the major branches of the Union forces—infantry, cavalry, artillery, and navy— which are one-third larger than life and heroic in conception. For the infantry, "The Color Guard," depicts an actual incident during the Battle of Resaca. "Mortar Practice," the naval group, includes an African American sailor, one of the few blacks to be represented on Civil War monuments of the period.

Inside the monument's base is a sizable memorial room surrounding the bottom of the shaft. Around the central core are four bronze panels in bas-relief depicting various aspects of the Civil War. "The Beginning of the War in Ohio" is dominated by the state's three war governors: William Dennison, David Tod, and John Brough. Another panel depicts Lincoln placing a rifle in the hands of an emancipated slave. Lincoln and his generals is the subject of "The Peacemakers at City Point." Finally, the southern panel memorializes the women of the Northern Ohio Soldiers' Aid Society and the Hospital Service.

But the true heart of the monument appears on the exterior walls facing the panels. There, grouped by regiments, are carved in marble the names of Cuyahoga County's 10,000 Civil War veterans, most of them compiled by Mrs. Scofield. Above the south entrance to the room is a couplet composed by the secretary of the Monument Commission, Levi F. Bauder:

Break ranks and rest till the last trumpet's call
Shall sound the fateful reveille for all.

Their rest has not been entirely undisturbed, as the monument has attracted its share of detractors through the years. "It's a monstrosity," said Charles C. Curran,

secretary of the National Academy of Design in 1925. "The only thing you can do is cover it with ivy." An anonymous visitor from Boston a decade later called it an "outrage" and sent a contribution of one dollar to the *Cleveland Press* toward a campaign to tear it apart "stone by sculpture, and plop it into Lake Erie." During World War II a patriotic newspaper columnist suggested that the statuary be donated as scrap metal for the war effort. These attacks seemed to recur every decade. In 1959 an architect got so tired of seeing it from his office window on Public Square that he petitioned the state legislature, unsuccessfully, to have it moved to Garfield Park. Architect Scofield, perhaps learning a lesson from the fate of the Perry Monument, had been wise in designing one so difficult to relocate. By the time of its centennial in 1994, the Soldiers' and Sailors' Monument had achieved acceptance as both a Cleveland and a national landmark. "I think this is one of the most important Civil War monuments in the country," said historian James McPherson at its birthday celebration. "It's certainly one of the largest and most impressive."[15]

Since 1894 the Soldiers' and Sailors' Monument has endured for more than a century as one of Cleveland's most recognized, revered, and even sometimes maligned landmarks. It is seen here decorated for a GAR (Grand Army of the Republic) convention in 1901.

And so it endures, as do the names of the memorialized. In the background of "The Peacemakers at City Point" panel inside appears Maj. Gen. Mortimer D. Leggett, husband of diarist Marilla Leggett. Rebecca Rouse may be seen on the panel dedicated to the Soldiers' Aid Society, along with Ellen Terry and Mary Clark Brayton. Listed on the facing walls under the 1st OVI is the unfortunate Alexander Varian, who made the ultimate sacrifice at Resaca. Both Morris Holly and Franklin Rockefeller may be found under the 7th OVI. Col. Oliver H. Payne appears at the head of the 124th OVI, which he commanded. And although Frank Rieley had gone outside the county to enlist in the 3rd Ohio Cavalry, his name too was added to a later panel.

Cleveland's Soldiers' and Sailors' Monument has its smaller counterparts in dozens of towns and county seats of northern Ohio. They all endure in mute but eloquent testimony to the region's experiences, contributions, and sacrifices in the American Civil War.

Notes

PROLOGUE

1. *Annals of Cleveland, 1818–1935,* vol. 43, 1860 (Cleveland: WPA Project 14066, 1937), no. 426.

2. William Ganson Rose, *Cleveland: The Making of a City* (Cleveland: World Publishing Company, 1950), 222.

3. *Cleveland Leader,* July 18, 1860.

4. *Leader,* Mar. 5, 1861.

5. *Annals,* 1860, no. 995.

6. *Leader,* Mar. 5, 1861.

7. [George B. Senter], *Mayor's Address, to the City Council of the City of Cleveland* (Cleveland: Fairbanks, Benedict, 1861), 10.

8. *Leader,* Sept. 11, 1860.

9. Ibid.

10. *Annals,* 1860, no. 1345.

11. Ibid., no. 1347.

12. Ibid.

13. Herbert Croly, *Marcus Alonzo Hanna: His Life and Work* (New York: Macmillan, 1912), 37.

14. Ibid.

1. THE GATHERING STORM

1. Mary Harrison Games, *The Underground Railroad in Ohio* (ca. 1937), 112.

2. Allan Peskin, ed., *North into Freedom: The Autobiography of John Malvin, Free Negro, 1795–1880* (Kent, Ohio: Kent State Univ. Press, 1988), 30.

3. Ibid., 32–33.

4. *The Aliened American* (Cleveland), Apr. 9, 1853.

5. Ibid.

6. Harry James Brown and Frederick D. Williams, eds., *The Diary of James A. Garfield,* vol. 1, 1848–1871 (East Lansing: Michigan State Univ. Press, 1967), 344–45.

7. Jacob R. Shipherd, comp., *History of the Oberlin-Wellington Rescue* (1859; New York: Negro Univ. Press, 1969), 62.

8. Ibid., 81.

9. Ibid., 177.

10. Ibid., 178.

11. *Cleveland Plain Dealer*, May 22, 1860.

12. *Plain Dealer,* June 25, 1860.

13. *Leader*, Nov. 8, 1860.

2. "IT WILL BE A SHORT WAR"

1. *Plain Dealer*, Dec. 21, 1860.

2. Allan Nevins, *John D. Rockefeller: The Heroic Age of American Enterprise* (New York: Scribner's, 1940), 1:138.

3. *Leader*, Jan. 22, 1861.

4. *Leader,* Jan. 24, 1861.

5. *Plain Dealer*, Jan. 23, 1861.

6. *Leader*, Feb. 25, 1861

7. *Astabula Sentinel,* Jan. 30, 1861.

8. *Annals*, 1861, no. 3399.

9. *Leader*, Feb. 13, 1861.

10. *Leader*, Feb. 14, 1861.

11. *Plain Dealer*, Feb. 15, 1861.

12. *Leader*, Feb. 16, 1861.

13. Ibid.

14. *Leader*, Feb. 15, 1861.

15. *Leader*, Feb. 18, 1861.

16. Albert Gallatin Riddle, *Recollections of War Times: Reminiscences of Men and Events in Washington, 1860–1865* (New York: Putnam's, 1895), 14.

17. Ibid.

18. Jacob Donelson Cox, *Military Reminiscences of the Civil War* (New York: Scribner's, 1900), 1:2.

19. James A. Garfield Papers, Library of Congress, Series 5.

20. *Leader*, Apr. 13, 1861.

21. *Plain Dealer*, Apr. 13, 1861.

22. *Leader*, Apr. 15, 1861.

23. Ibid

24. *Leader*, Apr. 18, 1861.

25. *Annals*, 1861, no. 586.

26. Ibid., no. 587.

27. Nevins, *John D. Rockefeller*, 1:139.

28. Grace Goulder, *John D. Rockefeller: The Cleveland Years* (Cleveland: Western Reserve Historical Society [WRHS], 1972), 57.

29. Caroline Younglove Abbot, typescript memoir, p. 2, U.S. Sanitary Commission Records, WRHS.

30. [M. C. Brayton and E. F. Terry], *Our Acre and Its Harvest: Historical Sketch of the Soldiers' Aid Society of Northern Ohio* (Cleveland: Fairbanks, Benedict, 1869), 20.

31. Ibid., 20–21.

32. Ibid., 21.

33. Riddle, *Recollections,* 44–45.

34. Ibid., 50–51.

35. *Leader*, July 31, 1861.

3. THE HARD ROAD TO FREEDOM

1. Riddle, *Recollections of War Times,* 41–43.

2. Sept. 5, 1861, Frank Rieley Correspondence, WRHS.

3. Sept. 27, 1861, Rieley Correspondence.

4. Sept. 3, 1861, Alexander Varian Jr. Letters, Western Reserve Historical Society, Cleveland.

5. Sept. 6, 1861, Alexander Varian Jr. Letters.

6. Sept. 8, 1861, Alexander Varian Jr. Letters.

7. Oct. 3, 1861, Col. Oliver H. Payne Letters, transcribed by Roderick Boyd Porter, the Payne Fund Archives, Cleveland.

8. Apr. 21, 1861, Oliver Payne Letters.

9. Oct. 3, 1861, Oliver Payne Letters.

10. Oct. 21, 1861, Oliver Payne Letters.

11. Mar. 3, 1862, Oliver Payne Letters.

12. Oct. 19, 1861, Rieley Correspondence.

13. Jan. 20, 1862, Rieley Correspondence.

14. June 25, 1861, Morris I. Holly Letters, WRHS.

15. Aug. 1, 1862, Oliver Payne Letters.

16. Mar. 17, 1862, Oliver Payne Letters.

17. Sept. 22, 1863, Oliver Payne Letters.

18. Sept. 28, 1863, Oliver Payne Letters.

19. Sept. 22, 1862, Morris Holly Letters.

20. July 4, 1863, Peter Marshall Hitchcock Family Papers, WRHS.

21. June 8, 1864, Oliver Payne Letters.

22. *Plain Dealer,* July 6, 1923.

23. Nov. 27, 1863, Alexander Varian Jr. Letters.

4. LIFE ON THE HOME FRONT

1. *Leader,* Jan. 16, 1863.

2. *Leader,* Jan. 17, 1863.

3. *Plain Dealer,* Nov. 15, 1861.

4. [Charles F. Brown], *Artemus Ward: His Book* (New York: Carleton, 1862), 64–68.

5. Ibid., 34–35.

6. [I. U. Masters], *Mayor's Address to the City Council of the City of Cleveland* (Cleveland: Fairbanks, Benedict, 1864), 5–6.

7. Nov. 29, 1863, Bingham Family Papers, the Payne Fund Archives, Cleveland.

8. Apr. 26, 1861, Nancie Swan Foskett Diaries, WRHS.

9. May 2, 1861, Nancie Swan Foskett Diaries.

10. July 29, 1861, Nancie Swan Foskett Diaries.

11. Sept. 29, 1861, Nancie Swan Foskett Diaries.

12. Nov. 16, 1862, Nancie Swan Foskett Diaries.

13. Mar. 8, 1863, Nancie Swan Foskett Diaries.

14. Apr. 3, 1863, Nancie Swan Foskett Diaries.

15. Mar. 15, 1863, Nancie Swan Foskett Diaries.

16. Sept. 13, 1863, Nancie Swan Foskett Diaries.

17. Feb. 11, 1862, Marilla Wells Leggett Diaries, WRHS.

18. Feb. 15, 1862, Marilla Wells Leggett Diaries.

19. Feb. 17, 1862, Marilla Wells Leggett Diaries.

20. May 30, 1863, Marilla Wells Leggett Diaries.

21. June 4, 1863, Marilla Wells Leggett Diaries.

22. Caroline Younglove Abbott, typescript memoir, U.S. Sanitary Commission Records, WRHS.

23. Ibid. 5.

24. Ibid. 4.

25. Brayton and Terry, *Our Acre and Its Harvest*, 62.

26. Ibid., 110.

27. May 17, 1863, Oliver Payne Letters.

28. Abbott, typescript memoir, 9–10.

29. Brayton and Terry, *Our Acre and Its Harvest*, 131.

30. Ibid., 136–37.

31. *Leader*, Feb. 24, 1864.

32. Brayton and Terry, *Our Acre and Its Harvest*, 189.

33. Ibid., 187.

34. *Leader*, Feb. 22, 1864.

35. Feb. 27, 1864, Oliver Payne Letters.

36. Marian J. Morton, *Women in Cleveland: An Illustrated History* (Bloomington: Indiana Univ. Press, 1995), 22.

5. BUSINESS AND POLITICS—BUT NOT AS USUAL

1. July 6, 1864, Oliver Payne Letters.

2. Feb. 27, 1864, Oliver Payne Letters.

3. July 16, 1864, Oliver Payne Letters.

4. Rachel Sherman Thorndike, ed., *The Sherman Letters: Correspondence between General and Senator Sherman from 1837 to 1891* (New York: Scribner's, 1894), 258.

5. Rose, *Cleveland*, 316.

6. Allan Nevins, *The War for the Union* (New York: Scribner's, 1959–71), 1:252.

7. June 29, 1864, Oliver Payne Letters.

8. Croly, *Marcus Alonzo Hanna*, 46.

9. Ibid., 47.

10. Goulder, *John D. Rockefeller*, 58.

11. Nevins, *John D. Rockefeller*, 1:180–81.

12. Croly, *Marcus Alonzo Hanna*, 49.

13. *Leader*, Nov. 1, 1865.

14. George W. Julian, *The Life of Joshua R. Giddings* (Chicago: A. C. McClurg, 1892), 385.

15. *Sentinel*, May 13, 1861.

16. Charles Richards Williams, ed., *Diary and Letters of Rutherford B. Hayes* (Columbus: Ohio State Archaeological and Historical Society, 1922), 2:163.

17. Theodore Clark Smith, *The Life and Times of James Abram Garfield* (New Haven, Conn.: Yale Univ. Press, 1925), 1:225.

18. *Sentinel*, Nov. 20, 1861.

19. *Sentinel*, Feb. 12, 1862.

20. *Leader*, Feb. 14, 1862.

21. Harvey S. Ford, ed., *Civil War Letters of Petroleum V. Nasby* (Columbus: Ohio State Univ. Press, 1962), 10–12.

22. *The Crisis* (Columbus, Ohio), July 2, 1862.

23. *Plain Dealer*, Oct. 13, 1862.

24. *Plain Dealer*, Oct. 16, 1862.

25. *Cincinnati Enquirer*, Oct. 17, 1862.

26. *Leader*, Jan. 3, 1863.

27. *Sentinel*, Jan. 7, 1863.

28. *The Crisis*, Jan. 7, 1863.

29. May 18, 1863, Oliver Payne Letters.

30. *Leader*, May 23, 1864.

31. Nevins, *War for the Union*, 4:104.

32. *Annals*, 1864, no. 2000.

33. Ibid., 1865, 51.

34. *Leader*, June 29, 1863.

35. *Leader*, July 1, 1863.

36. *Leader*, Aug. 6, 1863.

37. Apr. 4, 1865, Joseph William Briggs Papers, WRHS.

38. *Leader*, June 27, 1864.

39. *Annual Statement of the Trade, Commerce and Manufactures of the City of Cleveland, for the Year 1865* (Cleveland: Fairbanks, Benedict, 1866), 7–8.

EPILOGUE

1. Riddle, *Recollections of War Times*, 331–32.

2. Apr. 17, 1865, Rieley Correspondence.

3. *Leader*, Apr. 15, 1865.

4. *Leader*, Apr. 17, 1865.

5. *Leader*, Apr. 29, 1865.

6. *Herald*, Apr. 29, 1865.

7. *Herald*, Apr. 28, 1865.

8. Brayton and Terry, *Our Acre and Its Harvest*, 245.

9. Ella Grant Wilson, *Famous Old Euclid Avenue of Cleveland* (privately published, 1932), 24.

10. *Herald*, Apr. 29, 1865.

11. *Leader*, Apr. 29, 1865.

12. *Herald*, Apr. 29, 1865.

13. *Cleveland Press*, July 5, 1894.

14. *Leader*, July 5, 1894.

15. *Plain Dealer*, July 3, 1994.

Bibliography

MANUSCRIPT SOURCES

Caroline Younglove Abbott. Typescript memoir. U.S. Sanitary Commission Records. Western Reserve Historical Society (WRHS), Cleveland

Joseph William Briggs Papers. WRHS

Nancie Swan Foskett Diaries. WRHS

James A. Garfield Papers. Library of Congress, Washington, D.C.

Peter Marshall Hitchcock Family Papers. WRHS

Morris I. Holly Letters. WRHS

Marilla Wells Leggett Diaries. WRHS

Col. Oliver H. Payne Letters. Transcribed by Roderick Boyd Porter. The Payne Fund Archives, Cleveland, Ohio

Frank Rieley Correspondence. WRHS

Alexander Varien Jr. Letters. WRHS

NEWSPAPERS

The Aliened American (Cleveland)

Ashtabula Sentinel

Cincinnati Enquirer

Cleveland Herald

Cleveland Leader

Cleveland Plain Dealer

Cleveland Press

The Crisis (Columbus)

PUBLISHED SOURCES

PRIMARY SOURCES

Annual Statement of the Trade, Commerce and Manufactures of the City of Cleveland, for the Year 1865. Cleveland: Fairbanks, Benedict, 1866.

[Brayton, M. C., and E. F. Terry.] *Our Acre and Its Harvest: Historical Sketch of the Soldiers' Aid Society of Northern Ohio.* Cleveland: Fairbanks, Benedict, 1869.

Brown, Harry James, and Frederick D. Williams, eds. *The Diary of James A. Garfield: Vol. 1, 1848–1871.* Lansing: Michigan State Univ. Press, 1967.

[Browne, Charles F.] *Artemus Ward: His Book.* New York: Carleton, 1862.

Cox, Jacob Dolson. *Military Reminiscences of the Civil War.* 2 vols. New York: Scribner's, 1900.

Ford, Harvey S., ed. *Civil War Letters of Petroleum V. Nasby.* Columbus: Ohio State Univ. Press, 1962.

[Masters, I. U.] *Mayor's Address to the City Council of the City of Cleveland . . .* Cleveland: Fairbanks, Benedict, 1864.

Peskin, Allan, ed. *North into Freedom: The Autobiography of John Malvin, Free Negro, 1795–1880.* Kent, Ohio: Kent State Univ. Press, 1988.

Riddle, Albert Gallatin. *Recollections of War Times: Reminiscences of Men and Events in Washington, 1860–1865.* New York: Putnam's, 1895.

[Senter, George B.] *Mayor's Address, to the City Council of the City of Cleveland . . .* Cleveland: Fairbanks, Benedict, 1861.

Shipherd, Jacob R., comp. *History of the Oberlin-Wellington Rescue.* 1859. New York: Negro Univ. Press, 1969.

Thorndike, Rachel Sherman, ed. *The Sherman Letters: Correspondence between General and Senator Sherman from 1837 to 1891.* New York: Scribner's, 1894.

Williams, Charles Richard, ed. *Diary and Letters of Rutherford B. Hayes.* 5 vols. Columbus: Ohio State Archaeological and Historical Society, 1922.

Wilson, Ella Grant. *Famous Old Euclid Avenue of Cleveland.* Privately published, 1932.

SECONDARY SOURCES

Brandt, Nat. *The Town That Started the Civil War.* Syracuse, N.Y.: Syracuse Univ. Press, 1990.

Brief Historical Sketch of the Cuyahoga County Soldiers' and Sailors' Monument. Cleveland: Monument Commission, 1987.

Croly, Herbert. *Marcus Alonzo Hanna: His Life and Work.* New York: Macmillan, 1912.

Games, Mary Harrison. *The Underground Railroad in Ohio.* N.p., ca. 1937.

Goulder, Grace. *John D. Rockefeller: The Cleveland Years.* Cleveland: Western Reserve Historical Society, 1972.

Harper, Robert S. *The Ohio Press in the Civil War.* Columbus: Ohio State Univ. Press for the Ohio Historical Society, n.d.

Julian, George W. *The Life of Joshua R. Giddings.* Chicago: A. C. McClurg, 1892.

Morton, Marian J. *Women in Cleveland: An Illustrated History.* Bloomington: Indiana Univ. Press, 1995.

Nevins, Allan. *John D. Rockefeller: The Heroic Age of American Enterprise.* 2 vols. New York: Scribner's, 1940.

———. *The War for the Union.* 4 vols. New York: Scribner's, 1959–71.

Rose, William Ganson. *Cleveland: The Making of a City.* 1950. Kent, Ohio: Kent State Univ. Press, 1990.

Smith, Theodore Clark. *The Life and Times of James Abram Garfield.* 2 vols. New Haven, Conn.: Yale Univ. Press, 1925.

Stark, William C. "A Monumental Battle on Public Square." *Timeline* 20 (Jan.–Feb. 2003): 2–15.

Vacha, John E. "The Case of Sara Lucy Bagby: A Late Gesture." *Ohio History* 76 (Autumn 1967): 222–31.

Van Tassel, David D., and John J. Grabowski, eds. *The Encyclopedia of Cleveland History.* 2d ed. Bloomington: Indiana Univ. Press, 1996.

———. *The Dictionary of Cleveland Biography.* Bloomington: Indiana Univ. Press, 1996.

Index